Gallery Books
Editor Peter Fallon

THE ADAPTATIONS (1975-2020)

Derek Mahon

THE ADAPTATIONS

(1975-2020)

Gallery Books

The Adaptations (1975-2020)
is first published
simultaneously in paperback
and in a clothbound edition
on 31 May 2022.

The Gallery Press
Loughcrew
Oldcastle
County Meath
Ireland

www.gallerypress.com

ISBN 978 1 91133 842 0 *paperback*
978 1 91133 843 7 *clothbound*

A CIP catalogue record for this book
is available from the British Library.

The Adaptations (1975-2020) receives financial assistance
from the Arts Councils of Ireland.

Contents

for Rory, Katie and Maisie
and for Sarah

Chorus from *Antigone*

from the Greek of Sophocles, 496-406 BC

Wonders are many and none
more wonderful than man
whose sail and plunging prow
cleave a windswept path
through life-threatening seas;
who opens the rich earth
year after year with his
worn-out, unwavering plough.

Our visionary technology
outwits the throbbing thrush,
creatures of land and sea,
the bear and octopus,
and tames the ravening beast
in thicket and upland gorse.
A lion bites the dust;
we bridle the wild horse.

Our wide-ranging resources,
so beneficial, can also
serve evil purposes.
We honour those who show
due reverence to the divine
but spurn the sinful man:
blinded by his own pride,
he walks a lonely road.

With speech and intuitions
born in the lightning brain
we create civilizations,
shelter from wind and rain;

each difficult circumstance,
crisis, disease or pain,
inspires us. Only against
death do we strive in vain.

Chorus from Oedipus at Colonus

from the Greek of Sophocles

This here is Colonus' glittering town
known everywhere for horses, known
for its fine ships, where nightingales
sing in our quiet glades and hills,
the warm peace of our ivy glens,
in arbours hung with fruit and vines
out of the burning sun, and glimpse
the goat god with his naked nymphs.

Bathed in the dew of morning skies,
grave asphodels with shining eyes
sprinkle the forest floor and bright
crocuses blink in shafts of light.
Sparkling springs bubble and boil
down to the fields and drinking soil,
nourishing with their ample flow
the rich loins of the earth below.

With song and dance the Muses thrive
and teach the people how to live;
the dark-eyed olive flourishes here
in greater abundance than elsewhere,
its shade the school each student knows,
its woods a shield against our foes,
self-sown, self-grown and self-reliant,
watched by Athene day and night.

The horse, though, is our chief resource,
Poseidon's gift to us, the horse
and the white horses of the sea
we tamed here in our infancy

with bit and bridle, sail and oar,
on the high road and foaming shore;
and still we ride the salt sea wind
as in the first days of mankind.

Chorus from The Birds

from the Greek of Aristophanes c.446-c.386 BC

O troubled people, frantic creatures of an hour,
swift generations, curious growths that flower
and fade in a brief stretch of time as if
you haven't strength to live a longer life!
Dream shadows, listen to us, the sovereign birds,
students of the eternal whose wise words
can teach you everything there is to teach.
(Not even Pythagoras had our intuitive reach.)
Once there was night and chaos, empty space,
until an extraordinary event took place.
A shape formed in the darkness, an ovoid
laid by a loving spirit in the void;
love hatched the first birds and so life arose
with shiny wings and feathers, beaks and toes.
That's when the earth began, the sea and sky
and the capricious gods who never die.
We warbled, chirped and squawked, filling the air
with our fresh voices, audible everywhere.
Born of love, we have the wings of love,
the wings of doves, to swoop down from above
and inspire lovers when they want a ride.
Just think of the great service we provide!
Robin and nightingale, owl, wren and plover,
we're hugger-mugger with the human lover
who comes to the window, into the love nest
and snuggles up there to a stippled breast.
We mark the seasons, autumn, winter, spring . . .
Our vast migrations, on impatient wing,
remind you when to plough, to sow and reap,
when to pasture the herds and shear the sheep.
Muses, oracles, prophets, we supervise
your lives from our perspective in the skies.

Consider us your gods and we can promise you
longevity, world peace, increasing revenue,
plenty of stuff, and enough fluff to choke
the most priapic till the day you croak.

On Clouds

from the Latin of Lucretius (Titus Lucretius Carus), 98-c.55 BC,
De Rerum Natura VI, 451-526

Clouds take shape in the blue skies and gather
where flying bodies get tangled up together
and tiny clouds are blown along by breezes
till the moment when a stronger current rises.
Hills, for instance: the higher up the peak
the more industriously they seem to smoke;
wind blows these wisps on to the mountain tops
while they are still vague, evanescent strips
and there, heaped up in greater quantity,
they reveal themselves as a visible entity
trailing from snowy summits into the ether,
the empyrean spaces torn by wind and weather.
Steam rises from the sea, as becomes clear
when clothes on the shore absorb the salty air;
particles rise from rivers and wet slopes
while the sky, weighing upon them, packs them tight
and weaves them closely like a linen sheet.
Some come from space, as I've explained before,
their number infinite, their source obscure,
and these can travel at the speed of light.
No wonder the storm clouds, so fast and thick,
darkening fields and sea, slide up so quick
since from the blow-holes of the outer spheres,
as in our own windpipes, our veins and pores,
the elements come and go, strange and opaque,
through ducts and channels, rooms and corridors
as if in a house of opening, closing doors.
As for the rain clouds, how they come to grow
and fall as showers on the hard earth below —
a multitude of life-germs, water sperm, unites
with cloud stuff and secretions of all sorts,
heavy and dark, ice crystals and whatever

solution is in the clouds themselves, cloud water,
as our own bodies grow with the serum, gism,
sweat, whatever fluid is in the organism;
also they draw up brine with flowing sieves
when wind drives the clouds over the waves,
hoisting it from the surface in streaming fleeces
(same thing with bogs and other soggy places).
When all these water sources come together
clouds shed the excess moisture in their glands
by ganging up in a bunch to crush each other
till tears flow; or else, blown thin by winds
and sun-struck, they give off sizzling drops
as wax held to a brazier melts and drips.
Sometimes the two things coincide of course,
the violent pushing and the rushing wind-force,
and then you get a cloudburst which persists
with clouds upon clouds, tempests upon tempests
bucketing down and soaking the smoky air
while the earth exhales in bubbles everywhere.

How to Live

from the Latin of Horace (Quintus Horatius Flaccus), 65-8 BC,
Odes I, ii

Don't waste your time, Leucónoë, living in fear and hope
of the imprevisible future; forget the horoscope.
Accept whatever happens. Whether the gods allow
us fifty winters more or drop us at this one now
which flings the high Tyrrhenian waves on the stone piers,
decant your wine; the days are more fun than the years
which pass us by while we discuss them. Act with zest
one day at a time, and never mind the rest.

A Night with Cynthia

from the Latin of Sextus Propertius, c.50-c.16 BC

What a great woman, what an amazing night —
    so much ingenious turmoil in the bed.
I've never been the sort to lose my head,
    Cynthia, but our raptures in the lamplight,
eyes in adoring eyes, the murmured words . . .
    You fought bare-breasted or you drove me mad
with hot frustration keeping on your shirt;
    if I dozed off you'd bring me round again
with 'Wake up, lover, time to rise and shine.'
    And the wild mysteries, the talk afterwards!

We have to *see*. Strip or I rip your clothes
    to get you in the nip (there will be bruises),
for a long night will come when none may stare.
    Bind us for ever like demented doves
and set no limits to the love we share.
    Wheat will be knotweed, a black sun will rise
and wide rivers run back to their sources
    before I give an equal love to others.
No, I am yours in life and in death yours.

If the world lived like us instead of *them*
    — at amorous peace, rosy with wine and lust —
there would be no more war, no Roman dead
    bobbing up in the waves off Actium:
we do no harm when *we* fight limb for limb.
    Gather the roses while the roses last
since we can't know, euphoric in our pride,
    how present love may wither and decline
like dropped petals afloat in bowls of wine.

Epic Love

from the Latin of Sextus Propertius

Ponticus, while you pontificate about Thebes
    and internecine strife in the House of Atreus —
even rivalling Homer when in your singing robes
    if the Muses look kindly upon your verse —
we love poets prefer to write about love.
    Our judge is a wise, discriminating mistress.
I don't praise the brave tactical initiative;
    the heroism of lovers is my business.

No word from an epic or historical Muse.
    My inspiration is a young woman of taste:
light gown, deft hands, red shoes or a stray look
    speak volumes, and her eyes are an open book.
Thrown naked in the sack we two compose
    a private *Iliad*, epic enough for us —
so don't disparage love poetry, Ponticus,
    to please her with my rhymes is the greater test.

It's not only her looks that I admire,
    her high spirits and daunting literacy,
but how she listens when I read to her,
    head in her lap, and offers me her frank
and no-holds-barred reaction. If she likes
    my work I don't care what the others think:
her good opinion is enough for me
    though Jove himself line up with my worst critics.

Love Not War

from the Latin of Sextus Propertius

Augustus aims to raid the wealth of India,
    our oars will strike her pearl-providing sea.
Great victories there, rich pickings in the East!
    Indus will flow at the imperial whim.
One of these mornings I expect to see
    our wagons groaning with the spoils of war
and read the stickers — 'Patna', 'Kandahar' —
    while I recline upon my Cynthia's breast.

Though not rich, I prefer not war but love
    (wrestling with Cynthia is war enough)
but brawn beats brain in our unbalanced nature;
    the mind comes second in the human creature.
Of course, a poet isn't mad for gold,
    silver and precious stones, nor is he wild
to nick antiquities from conquered cities:
    he cultivates superior priorities.
Wind in their sails, the legions go to fight
    so the arms trade can show a healthy profit.

Expect to die poor, Sextus, but reflect —
    winners and losers will be spirits both.
When lovemaking ends with advancing years
    and a white snow lies on my thinning hairs
I'll spend my old age studying natural things,
    the lunar cycle and the wind direction,
the close relationship of clouds and springs
    and the spiritual economics of life on Earth.

The Midnight Note

from the Latin of Sextus Propertius

It's midnight and a note arrives from Tivoli —
    Cynthia requires my immediate presence there
where two white outcrops shine above the valley
    and generous pools shimmer with Anio's nymphs.
What to do? Trust myself to the fog and mist?
    Bandits? But there are worse things than murder.
It would be foolish to ignore this order
    however much I hate the midnight air.
Once when I failed her I was barred for months:
    my lady rules me with an iron fist.

Besides, lovers are special; nobody bothers us.
    We can walk unmolested down any street
or roam at will among the Scythian wilds.
    We pass unharmed through any neighbourhood:
who wants to be splattered with a lover's blood?
    The moon and stars illuminate our path,
the hostile terriers of farms and fields
    are dumb, our journeys blithe by day and night.
We have no need to fear a violent death,
    Venus herself is watching over us.

But even if I should get it in the neck
    I don't mind going through it for *her* sake.
She will burn incense, decorate my grave
    with wreaths, and sit there whimpering for days,
won't she? Not in one of those crowded cemeteries
    busy with people, loud with traffic noises.
No, plant me beneath trees in some quiet glade
    under an unmarked heap of earth and gravel
where I won't be one more name on the public road
    with casual strangers pissing on my ashes.

To Cynthia in the Country

from the Latin of Sextus Propertius

It grieves me that you've left me here in Rome.
    Still, I'm relieved you're in a rural spot
far from sexual predators. The countryside,
    innocent of intrigue, is the place to hide:
no rivals will be fighting outside your cot
    or shouting up at all hours of the night.
Alone without me, do you spend your time
    gazing at fields and farms? A restful sight.

With no playhouses to distract your mind
    you can watch men ploughing for hours on end
and skilful hands encouraging the vine.
    I can just see you kneel at a rough shrine,
unlike the temples where we often play,
    or hitching up your skirt for a good *céilí*
(though not enough to invite disrespect).
    You know, I think I'll join you there in fact.

I fancy a bit of sport, striding a hill,
    working with hounds in woods I used to know
like young Actaeon before he came to grief,
    and hanging skins on trees after a kill.
No lion, no wild boar, not on your life!
    No, I'll confine myself to hares and pigeons
where sweet Clitumnus' crystal stream begins
    and white oxen drink from the gentle flow.

Meanwhile if you feel any strange temptations
    remember I'll be there in a day or two.

. . . And at Baiae

from the Latin of Sextus Propertius

While you're on holiday beside the sea
    at decadent By-Eye, do you think of me?
At night, for instance, do you replay our games
    or has some beach bum with inflated limbs
oiled up to you and taught you to forget
    the serious love of your devoted poet?

I like to think you're crewing a nice yacht
    and practising your breaststroke daily, not
sun-worshipping on a secluded stretch of shore
    nude as a mermaid, since a girl of your
warm temperament could prove an obvious mark
    for some dickhead adept at sexy talk.

You are my life, my home, my favourite place —
    without you I don't count for much. (Whenever
friends notice my serene or wretched form
    I tell them you're the cause.) Get back to Rome
before Baiae infects you with its fever:
    everyone knows those beaches are a disgrace.

Immortality

from the Latin of Sextus Propertius

Orpheus who charmed the birds out of the pines
    and Dionysus, who with his Lydian pipes
whistled up Bacchae, are my archetypes:
    is it any wonder the girls like my lines?
Though I've no fancy columns, no gold or ivory
    furniture in the house, no 'water features',
I too will be named a famous son of Rome;
    my bones will lie in no dishonoured tomb.
Egyptian pyramids in the starry sky
    and other wonders of the world will die
from dust storms and the work of centuries
    but poetry like mine will live for ever.

A Quiet Orgy

from the Latin of Sextus Propertius

Such infidelities I could no longer take
    without going mad, but I hit on a strategy
and had some girls in for a quiet orgy.
    Teia, who lives near the Tarpeian Rock
and livens up when she has wine on board,
    brought round two sisters and we sat out
in the night-scented garden behind the yard.
    They sang songs; a black boy played the flute.

Deaf to their singing, blind to their naked charms
    during strip poker in the fading light,
distracted, thinking of a different lover,
    I drank too much and knocked a table over —
when, suddenly, a hinge squeaked in the gate.
    Raised voices echoed from the inner rooms
and Cynthia came out, her dander up,
    hot-eyed and furious. I dropped a cup.

Raging, she went straight for poor Teia's scalp
    while everybody yelled '*Aiuto*! Help!'
Rome awoke, lamps were lit, the neighbours heard
    and angry shouts shattered the midnight peace.
The girls grabbed their discarded party gear
    and ran off shrieking down the empty road
while Cynthia crowed derisively in the rear —
    then, turning, smashed a fist into my face.

She tore at a shoulder, bit into the neck,
    ripping a shirt, and gave me two black eyes;
so I ate dirt and started to apologize.
    Said she, 'If you really want to have me back

here are the three conditions you must obey:
    no more swanning about like a fornicator,
no eyeing up other women at the theatre,
    no hanging around stage doors after the play.'

These were her harsh conditions. 'Right,' said I.
    Roaring with laughter, flush with victory,
now undisputed mistress of the place,
    she disinfected furniture and doors,
ordering me out of my hot drawers.
    After she'd changed the sheets and pillowcases
and whipped a cloud of sulphur round my ears
    we scrambled into the sack and made our peace.

Cynthia's Ghost

from the Latin of Sextus Propertius

Ghosts do exist, death's not the end of it,
    something escapes beyond the funeral pyre.
Cynthia's ashes sit in their fresh grave
    at Tivoli, but she came to me last night
as I lay fretting on my lonely pillow,
    her gown singed and her lips deathly pale,
the beryl ring now fused to her dead finger.
    Her hair still glimmered and the same fire
flashed from her eyes as when she was alive;
    her voice was the hoarse chuckle I remembered.

'It's me, shove over in the bed,' she said,
    'you who were nowhere near me when I died —
stricken with grief, sez you. Cheat! Lying sod!
    Had you been there you might have eased the pains
but no, you were too busy with your floozies;
    nor did I think much of the box you chose.
Were all our whispers nothing but hot air?
    What of those wakeful nights in the Subura
when we'd get so worked up on our way there
    we'd heat the streets with our shenanigans?

'Did it not occur to you to give instructions
    for the cortège to pause at your own porch?
Bastard, there were no lilies or libations
    from you, *you* threw no myrrh into my smoke.
A curious end: question my slaves. I'm sure
    they fed me poison, shredding the prescriptions;
but hot tongs to the arse will make them talk.
    As for that bloody Chloris, your new whore,
if your maids speak fondly of me, the bitch
    punishes them by giving them extra work.

'Since I inspired your books be mindful, please,
    of my nurse Parthenië in her declining years
who took good care of *me* at the end; and burn
    those new sex poems where my name appears.
Keep an eye on the ivy round my plinth,
    it spreads below and chokes the burial urn.
Beside clear Anio's leaves and hyacinths
    inscribe these simple words on my headstone:
"Here in Tiburtine earth lies golden Cynthia —
    another glory, Anio, for your shores."

'The Ivory Gates send fantasies. Don't scorn
    the dreams the gods send from the Gates of Horn
fanning our sleep without illusory hopes.
    At night we walk abroad, but our dim shapes
shuffle back down to Charon's raft at dawn
    on the cold Styx, and there he checks each one.
Other women can have you now but I'll
    bestride your bones for ever when they finish.'
A pause; smiling her old complicit smile
    she slipped away from my embrace and vanished.

Ovid in Love

from the Latin of Ovid (Publius Ovidius Naso), 43 BC-AD 17,
Amores I, v

The day being humid and my head
heavy, I stretched out on a bed.
The open window to the right
reflected woodland-watery light,
a keyed-up silence as of dawn
or dusk, the vibrant and uncertain
hour when a shy girl might strip
and dance serenely in the nip.
You entered in a muslin gown,
bare-footed, your thick braids undone,
a fabled goddess with an air
as if in heat yet debonair.
Aroused, I grabbed and roughly tore
until your gown squirmed on the floor.
At first you resisted, but like one
who knows resistance is in vain;
and, when you stood revealed, my eyes
feasted on shoulders, breasts and thighs.
I held you hard and down you slid
beside me, as we knew you would.
Oh, come to me again as then you did!

Amores II, xi

This strange sea-going craze began
with Jason; pine from Pelion,
weathered and shaped, was first to brave
the whirlpool and the whistling wave.
I wish the *Argo* had gone down
and seafaring remained unknown;

for now Corinna, scornful of
her safety and my vigilant love,
intends to tempt the winds and go
cruising among the treacherous blue
waters where no shade-giving ilex,
temple or marble pavement breaks
with its enlightened artistry
the harsh monotony of the sea.
Walk on the beach where you can hear
the whorled conch whisper in your ear;
dance in the foam, but never trust
the water higher than your waist.
I'm serious. Listen to those with real
experience of life under sail —
believe their frightening anecdotes
of rocks and gales and splintered boats.
You won't be able to change your mind
when once your ship is far from land
and the most sanguine seamen cease
their banter as the waves increase.
How pale you'd grow if Triton made
the waters crash around your head —
so much more comfortable ashore
reading, or practising the lyre!
Still, if you're quite determined, God
preserve you from a watery bed:
Nereus' nymphs would be disgraced
if my Corinna should be lost.
Think of me when your shrinking craft
is a poignant pinpoint in the afternoon, and again when homeward bound
with canvas straining in the wind.
I'll be the first one at the dock
to meet the ship that brings you back;

I'll carry you ashore and burn
thank-offerings for your safe return.
Right there we'll make a bed of sand,
a table of a sand dune, and
over the wine you'll give a vivid
sketch of the perils you survived —
how, faced with a tempestuous sea,
you hung on tight and thought of me!
Make it up if you like, as I
invent this pleasant fantasy . . .

Galatea

from the Latin of Ovid, Metamorphoses X, 245-277

Pygmalion lived for years alone
without a wife to call his own.
Meanwhile, ingeniously, he wrought
a maiden out of ivory, one
lovelier than any woman born,
and with this shape he fell in love.
Alive, she seemed, and apt to move
if modesty did not prevent —
so did his art conceal his art.
He gazed at her in wonderment
and felt her limbs to be quite sure
that she was ivory, nothing more.
Her 'skin' responded to his stroke
or so he thought; and so he spoke,
seized her, imagining his thick
fingers sank into her back,
and looked for bruises on the work.
He whispered gentle, loving words,
brought presents, shells and pebbles, birds
and flowers, things that please young girls;
he clothed her, putting diamond rings
on her white fingers, ropes of pearls
about her neck and breasts. These things
were gorgeous, certainly, although
the naked sculpture even more so.

     He laid her down on a bed spread
with sheets dyed a Tyrian red,
called her his lover, propped her head
among soft, feathery pillows as if
a statue might have sensuous life.
Now Venus' feast day was the date;
the island thronged to celebrate.

Heifers, their young horns freshly gilt,
had felt the death stroke to the hilt
in their soft necks, as white as snow,
and the air smoked with incense. Now
Pygmalion, having devoutly laid
gifts on the altar, shyly prayed:
'Gods, if it's true that you can give
anything, grant I may make love . . .'
Too shy to say 'the maid', he said,
'. . . to someone like my ivory maid!'
But Venus, there in person, knew
what he intended and, to show
that she approved, the altar flames
shot up into the air three times.
Hastening home, the impatient lover
ran to the maid and, leaning over,
embraced her there on her chaste couch.
Her skin seemed warmer to his touch;
his fingers felt her thighs, at which
the ivory grew soft between
his thumbs, as wax melts in the sun
and, gently worked by loving hands,
stretches, relaxes and expands.

He stood amazed, still doubtful, thought
himself mistaken, and then not;
inflamed, he stroked her thighs again
until the statue blushed! Each vein
fluttered as our protagonist,
pouring out thanks to Venus, thrust
his lips upon live lips at last.
The maid, feeling his kisses, raised
shy eyes to the sun and, in a glance,
saw daylight and his face at once.

The goddess, with her genial presence,
sanctioned the union and in time
a girl, Paphos, was born to them —
from whom the island takes its name.

Echo

from the Latin of Ovid, Metamorphoses III, 356-402

Echo, who can't speak first but answers back,
had a real body once, not just a voice.
Though she was talkative she couldn't talk
properly even then; she had no choice
but to re-echo others' phrases. Why?
Juno, when she might have surprised Jupiter
fooling with his nymphs on the mountainside,
was often tricked by Echo's cunning chatter
so that the girls skedaddled. Recognizing
the ruse, she came down hard on the cheeky thing:
'I'll soon put a stop to your prattling tongue' —
so, speaking others' words in the same tone,
Echo re-echoes the last words she's heard.
One day, seeing the lost boy in a wood,
she followed at a distance and fell for him.
The closer she got the livelier the heat
scorching her like a quick sulphurous flame.
She longed to articulate but nothing came
and so she waited for the boy to start.
'Anyone here?' said he; she answered, 'Here'.
He paused, surprised, gazing about, and cried,
'Oh come on!', hearing the echo cry, 'Come on!'
He looked behind but, seeing nobody there,
darkly he asked, 'Are you avoiding me?'
and heard his own words asking in reply.
Confused by the echo-voice he tried again:
'Talk to me!' — and the echo, 'Talk to me!'
(Never would she so ardently respond
to anything.) Now, stepping from behind
a tree, she goes to throw her arms around him.
Coldly he shakes her off, brusquely he leaves
saying, 'Keep off, I don't want your embraces,
don't touch me!' 'Touch me!' cries our heroine.

Stricken, she hid for shame among the leaves —
since when she prefers quiet, lonely places.
The love and pain stayed rooted in her breast,
the pain increasing as the love increased.
Dismal imaginings disturbed her sleep,
the moisture in her flesh evaporated.
She grew thin and wasted, her girly sap
sucked by the air until a voice alone
remained; the bones, stiffening, turned to stone,
so rumour has it. Now, though never seen
in the open, she can be heard by everyone:
the voice survives. Where? In a hollow cave,
in a valley, a forest clearing, a silent grove.

Ariadne on Naxos

from the Latin of Ovid, Heroides X

Above the cold beach and the pounding waves,
Theseus, your wretched Ariadne grieves.
(I write this in our hut behind the strand
with hidden birds chirping along the coast.)
You were worse than a beast, at least a beast
would have some pity for its own kind.
Abruptly waking, knowing you weren't here,
I scrambled up, struck by a sudden fear,
and ran down in time to see the sun rise
as your sail opened in the morning breeze.
Distraught and furious, my clothes undone,
I stood there shrieking like a madwoman
or some lost Maenad, while the waves rose
to thigh and hip; and there my heart froze
watching you go, me with my failing strength
who rescued you from the dark labyrinth.
There's no one here, no one to help me leave
this barren place, and even if there were
where would I go? I can't go home alive,
I who betrayed Crete to the foreigner.
Without my guidance and the spool of thread
I gave you in the maze, you would be dead.
'As long as we both live' was what you said.
We're both alive, I think, but not together
and now I know what the abandoned suffer.
Besides, I'm frightened that at any time
wolves may appear and tear me limb from limb
— or even men, who frighten me now too:
I've no faith left in people I don't know.
I wish I'd never saved your life back there.
Of course you overcame the Minotaur:
you'd no need of a shield to protect you,
not even those long horns could penetrate

a heart harder than flint, sharper than slate.
Am I to die here? Will my body lie
exposed to buzzards watching from the sky
or will some kind god take pity on me?
When you get home, famous, and at the dock
tell them the story of the Cretan cave
include the love your Ariadne gave
before you left her here on this bare rock.

Human Wishes

from the Latin of Juvenal (Decimus Junius Juvenalis),
c.AD 50-c.127, Satires X

No one in his right mind would want to be
a big fish gobbling up the smaller fry;
it's the big fish who attract hostility
like Seneca and the rest in Nero's day.
You're better off to sit tight in your room
than be conspiring in the rising steam
among the towels of the baths and gym;
take change if you go out walking after dark,
avoid the war zones and the periphery
and keep your wits about you in the park
where a knife gleams behind each shadowy tree.
All pursue riches in our modern Rome,
gardens, a coach house and a second home
bought with the revenue from untaxed income
at Capua, Aquinum, Trevignano or Tivoli;
but poison's seldom served in wooden cups.
Beware the crystal glass and golden bowl,
be careful when you raise wine to your lips
dining with colleagues on the Palatine Hill
or old friends in the Caffè Giovenal'
on swan and flamingo, antelope and stuff.
So which philosopher would we rather know
— the one who, staring from his portico,
laughs, or the one who weeps? Easy to laugh,
if we started weeping there'd be no end to it.
Democritus would shake with continual mirth,
even in his primitive times, at life on earth
and showed that stoicism spiced up with wit,
some candour and good sense, can mitigate
even the thick air of a provincial city.
Binge sex and fiscal heroin, discreet

turpitude flickering in a brazier light —
all anyone does now is fuck and shit;
instant gratification, entertainment, celebrity
we ask, but mumbling age comes even so,
the striking profile thick and stricken now,
the lazy tackle like a broken bough,
the simian features and the impatient heir.
What else can you expect from your white hair,
your voice like cinders under a kitchen door?
What use to you the glittering cleavages,
the best box in the house above the stage
when blind and deaf? Now fever and disease
run riot through our waste anatomies,
the old mind dithering in its anecdotage,
the joints all seizing up with rheumatism,
seek guidance of the heavenly gods who treasure
our lives more than we do ourselves. Subdued
by protocol and the fear of solitude,
you wed in haste and now repent at leisure
even as your hands shake in their final spasm.
Ask for a sound mind in a sound body
unfrightened of the grave and not demented
by grief at natural declension; study
acceptance in the face of fate; and if
you want to worship mere materialism,
that modern god we have ourselves invented,
I leave you to the delights of modern life.

from The Bangor Antiphonary

from the Latin (7th century), anonymous

Bangor the best example
disciplined and pious
we keep plain and simple,
grave but harmonious.

Our fortunate community,
founded in faith, prescribes
faith, hope and charity
to its priests and scribes.

It stands like a ship ashore
safe in its quiet haven,
like a young bride before
the High King of Heaven —

a rock-built house, a home
delightful to the eyes,
a vine imported from
old Egypt's monasteries.

Devout and dedicated,
our sanctuary is sound
and strongly situated
on its rising ground —

substantial too, an ark
blazing with golden things
and intricate metalwork:
cherubim, angel wings.

This chaste maiden mother
whose windows shine at night
immune to worldly bother,
simple yet erudite,

enfolds a Christian flock,
echoes with Latin hymns
and gleams like a castle rock
bright with exotic gems.

Beyond grief and anger
in this eternal home,
our life here in Bangor
prefigures the life to come.

RIVER OF STARS

The Long Road to Sichuan

from the Chinese of Li Po, 701-762

The long road to Sichuan, so steep and high,
is harder to climb than the road to heaven.
Ts'an Tsung and Yu Fu opened up this region
eight thousand years ago, crossing the Ch'in
border by paths known only to the raven,
and looked west where once the mountains split
and the earth crumpled. Many died; they built
tracks and bridges in a continuous chain
where six dragons rotate around the sun.
Even cranes find it hard to come this way,
the gibbons climb slowly and anxiously.
We scale the Pleiades and grasp Orion;
past rock and cliff we reach the barren moon
exhausted, and stretch out with a long sigh.
When will we ever get back? Jackdaw and crow
croak in the morning to an empty sky.
The long road to Sichuan, so steep and high,
is harder to climb than the road to heaven.
A blasted pine leans over a ravine
where cataracts and rapids boil below
and boulders crash down where we aim to go.
Cheng-du* provides some consolation, though
it's nothing to the going-home consolation.
The long road to Sichuan, so steep and high,
is harder to climb than the road to heaven.
I look to east and west with a long sigh.

*Sichuan capital

The War Zone

from the Chinese of Li Po

Above the Altai Mountains the moon rises
and drifts in a sea of cloud; a desert wind
blows down the valleys for a thousand miles.
The sons of Han march through Manchuria
while Tatars stare down from the Pamirs
at this old war zone where so many died.
Soldiers picture the homes they left behind
where anxious women watch from upper floors.

A Kettle of Wine

from the Chinese of Li Po

Sitting among flowers with a kettle of wine
I lift my cup and drink to the bright moon.
A party of three: the moon, my shadow and me.
The moon is no drinker, sadly; however
I toast the spring and the spring flowers.
When I sing my shadow bobs in the Yellow River,
when I dance the moonbeams in the water waver.
Sober, we are content here in a group;
when we get drunk my shadow and I break up.
To pledge eternal amity we gather
in cloud depths and in a river of stars.

The Thatched Hut

from the Chinese of Ch'iu Wei, 710-775

The road goes up for miles into the mountain
and here at the top is your thatched hut,
but nobody's at home and the door is shut.
Squinting through the window I see a plain
table, a simple chair. You must be out
walking, fishing perhaps: weaving about
like swifts, we fail to meet. I stand still
in the long grass shining with recent rain
as peace descends, startling the eye and ear
to something like an ecstatic trance.
When it recedes I go back down the hill:
there's no need to wait for you to appear,
I've understood your theory of existence.

A Shabby Welcome

from the Chinese of Tu Fu, 712-770

Springtime, pine scent, and the river in spate.
Only the seagulls visit our lonely home.
I realize as I open the garden gate
the path hasn't been swept: a shabby welcome.
So far from town we have no delicacies
and can offer only vegetarian dishes.
As you'd expect, we're too poor for wine
but somewhere I've a drop of old moonshine.

Thinking of Li Po

from the Chinese of Tu Fu

Severance caused by death is an end of life
but the lost living are a persistent grief.
No word from you in your harsh banishment
among the malarial swamps beyond Kiang-nan.
I think of the companionship we knew
and summon up your spirit, half afraid
you've vanished into everlasting shade —
but no, you're still alive though never seen,
caught in the web of politics. The moon
shining in through the windows of my house
seems to illuminate your remembered face.
The lakes are fathoms deep, the rivers wide
beneath immeasurable high-sailing cloud,
and breezes chop the Yangtse's rippling surface.
Don't lose the oars that always guided you!
(I've seen you in a dream scratching your old
white head like one forced to renounce his due.)
We still keep our elaborate routine
here in Ch'ang-an*; you languish in the cold.
I know your thoughts tonight so far from home,
old friend. I understand: eternal fame
is a poor consolation when life is done.

*T'ang capital

54

Autumn Fields

from the Chinese of Tu Fu

The autumn fields grow bleaker every day
and the streams colder as the sky changes.
We're living here in exile at K'uei-chou
among country people on the middle Yangtse.
Others will taste the fruits of my best years.
We cultivate our beans and cabbages;
I eat sparingly now in my old age
and throw our scraps to the local carp.

It's easy to understand the flow of life
where everything fulfils its own nature
with fish happiest in the deepest water
and birds most at home in the leafiest wood;
but worldly ambition is for younger men,
at my age I'm resigned to failing powers.
An autumn wind shivers my walking stick
but peace of mind resides in ferns, flowers,

music and daily habit for equilibrium,
regular exercise to keep up the strength.
I sit in the bamboo sunshine of my library,
a straw hat over my eyes, a student
of wind-blown pine cones, ants and midges,
trivial things we tend to ignore.
On my woodland walks I pause before
the scents of willowherb and water mint.

The sands are shining on the farther shore
and an evening glow crimsons the high ridges.
Slow-pulsing gills surprise the tripping ripples
and tired wings contend with a rising wind.

Sounds of washing come from the little bridges,
woodmen sing as they chop up the dead wood.
It's frosty now, with snow on the dark air;
white drifts will cut us off from the world.

My intention was to shine among the eagles
but it's ducks and geese I'm going down among.
The autumn river is in full spate:
I hear the thundering gorges roar at night.
The upland paths are blocked by strewn rubble
and timber; immense clouds obscure the sun.
My children chatter in the local tongue
and I can't see them prospering in Ch'ang-an.

The Bangor Blackbird

from the Old Irish (9th century), anonymous

Just audible over the waves
a blackbird among leaves
whistling to the bleak
lough from its whin beak.

Spring Song

from the Occitan of Guilhem IX d'Aquitaine, 1071-1127

At the first warmth of spring
the forest fills with leaves;
each bird in its own tongue
whistles a new tune:
time now to look again
at our own lives and loves.

She sends no word of hope
to set my heart at ease.
I neither laugh nor sleep
nor can I concentrate,
not knowing if the upshot
will be the one I choose.

Our love is a hawthorn branch
shaking at night against
a sky of wind and rain
until the rising sun
spreads itself and glows
among the leaves and boughs.

One morning sticks in the mind:
while we lay dim and fond
she made me the gift of her
intimacy and fervour.
Soon may my busy hand
be in her skirt for ever.

Cheap rumours left and right
threaten our fierce desire
and force us far apart.

Danger, what do we care?
No malice, no envious spite
can spoil the thing we share.

DAWN SONGS

Blue Skies

from the Occitan (12th century), anonymous

Just like the nightingale for ever
whistling fiercely to his lover
I whisper to you all night,
my whispering flower —
until from a high tower,
like a new voice, dawn light
announces the time to rise.
Day breaks with its blue skies.

On the Road

from the Occitan of Jaufré Rudel (?1120-1147)

When in spring the days grow long
I listen to birds' distant song;
out on the road again I go
crippled with vain desire,
losing her, to imagine
the hot wars of religion.
Neither bird nor mayflower
pleases me more than ice and snow.

WOMEN IN LOVE

from the Occitan (12th century)

TIBORS DES BAUX

Belovèd friend, believe me when I say
I haven't spent an undesirous day
since first I met and chose you for my love,
nor let an hour pass when I didn't give
some thought to you and that the most intense.
I've known no moment of regret or penitence;
nor, if you left me with an angry word,
have I had peace of mind till you returned.

ANONYMOUS (MARIE DE VENTADOUR?)

What I write now I write with grief and pain:
those troubadours of a previous generation,
dead now, committed a most grievous sin
and threw their epoch into dire confusion
when they were frankly critical of women;
for those who hear, believing their glib song,
decide there must be truth in the aspersion
and so perpetuate a serious wrong.

Those gentlemen, great poets though they be,
only pretended to be serious lovers
since he who speaks of love ambiguously
dishonours love and is a great deceiver.
And if, against the truth of his own nature,
he should deceive himself, it's his disgrace:
without a woman he can have no future;
the love of women is his best resource.

ANONYMOUS

Heart veiled in sorrow, I've made up my mind
to renounce love and love's society
since on this earth I never hope to find
a friend so genial and so fine as he.
He was courageous, honourable and clever,
so madly brave he died as a result:
if I should ever take another lover,
now he is gone, my heart would be at fault.

GARSENDA DE FORCALQUIER

You with the air of a whole-hearted lover,
I'm more than pleased you like me if you do;
I wish you wouldn't be so shy, however,
since I am similarly in love with you.
I know your modesty, your fiery blushes.
You hesitate to speak of what you feel;
but a woman daren't disclose her secret wishes
in words or action lest she seem a fool.

BÉATRICE DE DIE

Great pain has come to me
from a young man I lost.
Of the young men I know
I fancied him the most;
and now I've been betrayed
since I refused my love.
What was I thinking of,
lying there cold and hard?

If he should come again
I'd clasp him with my thighs
until he gasped for breath
and gravely take him in
since I would be his wife;
like some great heroine
I'd give him my bright eyes,
my heart, my soul, my life.

Dear friend, should you once more
decide to be my lover
and spend a night with me,
I'll love you ardently;
no pleasure can compare
with what we shall find there,
believe me, if you do
just what I ask you to.

ANONYMOUS

I walk alone in the green wood
with no friend at my side.
I lost him through ineptitude
and walk alone in the green wood.
I should write to let him know
I'll make it up to him somehow.
I walk alone in the green wood
with no friend at my side.

AZALAIS DE PORTIRAGNES

Winter is here, the frozen time
of frosty nights, of snow and slush;

the singing birds we love are dumb
and silent in the hawthorn bush.
Hedges are bare beside the road,
no leaf or flowering branch in sight;
there is no nightingale to be heard
who wakes the soul on a spring night.

My furious heart is so distraught
I am estranged from everyone;
I realize we lost the fight
more quickly than it takes to win.
We are at fault if we don't love
a man of honour, a man of worth;
I've lost the one who was my life
and mourn the fact from this day forth.

Bedroom

from the Italian of Petrarch, 1304-1374

The little bedroom, previously a haven
from daily tempests beating at my head,
is now a fountain basin for tears shed
I try to stifle out of shame and scorn.
Love, kind to others, harsh to me alone,
asperges every night the little bed,
hitherto my relief and consolation,
with mournful hands from a prodigious urn.

Of peace and privacy I don't fight shy
so much as the thoughts nesting in my brain
which, given scope, would often stretch and fly.
Now to my own surprise, for who'd've thought it,
I join that rowdy crowd I always hated
rather than find myself alone again.

Exequy

from the Italian of Petrarch

The eyes of which I spoke so warmly once,
the face and figure, shoulders, hands and knees
that once deranged my rational faculties
and made me different from the usual bunch;
the quick inviting smile and generous breast,
the streaming hair with its angelic glow
that seemed to make a paradise below,
are now a whisper of insentient dust.

Yet I live on, in grief and self-disdain,
bereft of the light I loved so earnestly,
as if on a lost ship in a storm at sea.
Now there will be no more love poetry:
the vital flow has dried up in the vein
and the strings whimper in a minor key.

Night and Day

from the Italian of Ludovico Ariosto, 1474-1533

Brighter and clearer to me than mere daylight
are crafty night-for-day and day-for-night
when sun and stars, conspiring with the dark,
relax their vigilance and fade to black.
Cloud cover, shadow; the world goes to bed
and leaves two lovers only wide awake,
one caped and hooded down a colonnade
furtively flitting on invisible wings
where a door opens with a faint squeak
audible only to the intent sex maniac.
I'm still not sure if I'm imagining things
when your hand guides me to a secret spot
where hips and thighs like vines reticulate,
I quench my thirst in your wide-open mouth,
we gasp the quick rush and exchange of breath
and tremble in the metaphysical love fight.
These images will persist until life cease,
exploding like the sulphurous candlelight
which showed us clearly what was taking place,
pre-coital fever and post-coital peace,
consensual chiaroscuro and thumping heart.
No love can be complete with the light out
— so much better to have the gaze rest
on gaze, flesh tones and cherishable breast,
the speaking ears, the flickering and the moist
and the rose-petal lips unknown to thorn,
so satisfying the senses that each one
comes into play and none is left forlorn.
So precious the night-time and so brief,
and so severe the hardships of this life
when day breaks, banishing your dozy lover,
can we not live in a world of love for ever?

Art and Dust

from the Italian of Michelangelo, 1475-1564

How can it be, as long experience shows,
the image hidden in the calcium carbonate
lasts longer, lady, than the artist does
who turns to dust again as at the start?
The cause yields to the outcome and withdraws;
nature is conquered once again by art
and, proving this, my very sculpture knows
death and time, faced with the work, depart.

A long life to the pair of us I can give
in either medium, whether in paint or stone,
to keep our living countenances alive
so people centuries after we have gone
will see your beauty and my wretched plight
and know in loving you I got it right.

Oisín

from the Irish (16th century), anonymous

Wind chimes on wave and wood.
Niamh, daughter of ocean,
knows the naive Oisín
has gone to his true reward.

An Aspiring Spirit

from the Spanish of Francisco de Quevedo, 1580-1645

The final dark can take away my eyesight,
obliterating the white blaze of day;
it can release my soul and maybe gratify
the anxious hope of an eternal light —

but even on the farther shore it won't deter
the thought of where my earthly being burned:
blithely ignoring the strict rules, my fond
desire will swim back through the icy water.

The life that held such an aspiring spirit,
the arteries that fed so much impatience,
the marrow once so glisteningly bright

may wither, but their ardour will survive.
There will be ashes, yes, but smouldering ashes;
there will be dust, but dust glowing with love.

The Young Cordwainer

from the French (17th century?), anonymous

I saw her standing there
beside the *porte-cochère.*
We're all in love with her:
which one will she prefer?
Good fortune would it be
did she decide on me.

I'm only a young cordwainer,
not some great landowner;
but, as I tie your shoe,
show me you like me too?
Oh, darling, be my lover
and live with me for ever.

On gleaming linen spread
in an enormous bed,
above our heads a knot
of twined forget-me-not,
we two shall sleep as one
till life itself is done.

A Game of Cards

from the Irish of Tadhg Ó Ruairc (fl. 1684)

Blánaid, I face you, gorgeous foe,
   girl of the wavy red chevelure,
each curl long and provocative
   reaching down to the forest floor.

Crazy about you, as you know,
   your grey eyes and lingering looks,
your round cheeks where roses glow,
   the eyebrows like two pen-strokes,

I listen to the languorous voice
   where your superior nature sings,
a finer sound than organ pipe
   or lute, sweeter than harp strings,

and dote upon your skilful hands,
   the long fingers and pink nails
designed to pluck a tremulous note
   or draw ink from quivering quills;

the perfect opalescent breast
   no knight or knave has ever known,
the slender body and slim waist:
   Blánaid, I play for you alone.

The game is up if I should glimpse
   a flash of knee or open side,
white ankle-flicker, pale instep,
   toes creamy as the incoming tide;

but take me with a daring move,
   bright woman of the devious mind.

Be generous with your secret love,
  relieve me of my dubious hand.

It beats me you can keep in check
  a cheat like me so quick to sin.
Strip poker, Scrabble, snap, bezique:
  whatever the game, we both can win.

So put your cards on the table, dear;
  shuffle the deck and shake the dice.
It's serious stakes we play for here
  and high time you showed your ace!

A Rewrite

from the Italian of Pietro Metastasio, 1698-1782

I invent dreams and stories, and even as I outline
dreams and romances on the unwritten page
I enter into them with so soft a heart
I weep at evils of my own design.
I've more sense when not deceived by art;
the creative spirit is quiet then and rage,
love, genuine emotions, spring for once
from real life and from felt experience.

Ah, but words on the page aren't the whole story
for all my hopes and fears are fictions too
and I live in a virtual fever of creation —
the years of my life have been imagination,
my days a dream; when we wake from history
may we find peace in the substance of the true.

Dichtung und Wahrheit

from the German of Johann Wolfgang von Goethe, 1749-1832

Why did you give us these insightful powers,
these clear presentiments of the future, so
we never trust implicitly in our love,
our real lives never simple and naive?
Why did you give us, fate, the intuition
to see into the other's secret fears
and, with all this peculiar urge to know,
discern the true nature of our relation?
So many uncomplaining people live
dumbly, ignorant of their own desires,

drifting obtusely here and there, in vain
flight from some unforeseen vicissitude,
exulting sometimes when the amazing sun
of unexpected fortune dawns again.
Only to us two, loving though we are,
is the reciprocal delight denied
of loving without each examining why
and seeing each other as we never were,
always in search of a dreamt-up felicity
and wavering before some dreamt-up fear.

Happy are those whom a dream satisfies,
vaguely content to remain unaware!
Each brief encounter of our conscious eyes
only confirms the knowing thoughts we share.
What lies in store for us, and how did fate
devise for us this bond, so pure and strict?
In a far-distant time, in another life,
you were my sister or perhaps my wife
and knew me then in each particular,
listening for my nerves' tiniest note.

You'd read me clearly at a single glance,
hard though I know I am to understand;
you'd spread composure on my feverish brain,
direct my crazy, wandering steps, and in
your warm arms I'd find peace and confidence,
there to bind up my self-inflicted wounds.
With an instinctive ease you'd hold me bound
and fill up many a dull day with delight.
What rapture could equal those afternoons
I stretched out in gratitude at your feet

or felt my heart beating against your breast,
my senses clear and the hot blood at rest?
What's left of this is just a memory,
an ambient memory now faint and adrift.
The old truth still survives between us two
but the new situation brings me grief.
We're only half alive, it seems to me,
and a bright day is twilight where we sit.
I thank heaven, at least capricious fate
can never change the precious past we knew.

To 'Young Werther'

from the German of Johann Wolfgang von Goethe

Once more you venture forth, lamented shade,
into the light of day, encountering me
quite amicably in a fresh-flowering glade
as if you lived again in your lost youth
when evening dew refreshed us both
and after our long hours of industry
sunset enchanted us with a last gleam.
Your choice was to resign, mine to persist;
you haven't missed much in the interim.
A life on earth seems like a happy destiny,

the day so glorious and the night so vast;
but, planted in this paradisal place,
we've hardly even started to embrace
the sun when instinct, in perverse contrast,
rouses at once a strange antipathy
now to ourselves, now to the world we see,
and neither fits the other as it might.
It's dark outside despite the inner light
and a fair prospect hides from a grim gaze;
it's there at hand and we don't realize.

We think we've found it when a woman's form
bewitches us with its particular charm.
A young man, happy as a child in spring,
steps out like very spring itself, amazed,
enraptured: who has done this thing?
He looks about him and the world is his;
an urgent impulse draws him on.
Nothing constrains him, neither hedge nor door;
like a bird skimming a forest, there
he hovers, circling around the loved one

while from the clear air he will soon disown
he seeks the loving glance that tames his heart.
But, warned too soon, perhaps too late, his flight
he knows is baffled and himself ensnared.
Parting is hard and again twice as hard;
years are requited in a single look
but a harsh separation marks the end.
You smile, rightly and ruefully, old friend,
since your conclusion made you known
when we honoured your sad history in a book.

Those whom you left behind for better or worse
tread once again the labyrinthine course
of human love, since there remains for them
the always troubling and unknown future —
death at the end of it. How pure
and sure it sounds when poets sing
to cheat the death these dramas bring!
Caught in such agonies, ourselves to blame
for mad romance, may it be given to us
to speak true of the trials we have to face.

Sceilg Bay

from the Irish of Tomás Rua Ó Súilleabháin, 1785-1848

One fine, soft morning — St. Michael's Day —
Communion-bound in the Sceilg Bay,
we watched as the breakers multiplied,
rain threatened and a strong wind blew.
We wisely decided on turning back
and finding harbour beyond Bray Head;
starting up when I heard the crew,
I who'd been dozing was wide awake.

Our seine-boat was a delight that morning,
high in the waves, six oars at work,
the sail full and the rowlocks slick,
every board alive and singing.
We'd held her fast in the flying foam
surging and sparkling beneath the beam;
no stir on the water from here to Dingle
until we made for St. Michael's Rock —

when Sow Cliff there on the port side
shrieked fit to be tied, Gull Sound
roared aloud like a bull in pain,
the Groaner groaned in the howling wind.
Thanks be to Jesus we weren't drowned
and stretched in the dark depths of the tide
but spared for another, quieter run
when, please God, we can try again.

The priest prayed loudly in the stern
to spare the boat and save the men,
and he must have been heard in heaven above
as the white wave-crests crashed over us
for we cleared Rincarragh in due course
with the Narrows a flat calm after the sea;

so we kept on till we came to shore
and broached a barrel at Seán Magee's.

God, we were shook, so we sat all night
and emptied the porter, watching the gale
from a warm room until first light
and giving thanks for our lucky escape.
Ribbed, tarred and finished by Seán O'Neill,
that little boat will never know harm:
where would you find a finer ship
to deliver you safe from such a storm?

Winter Morning

from the Russian of Alexander Pushkin, 1799-1837

A magic morning, frost and sun
while you, my love, dream on;
but it's time now to rise.
Open those dopey eyes,
yourself a morning star,
and wake to a northern dawn.

After the wind last night,
when a thick fog came down
and, a mere yellow blur,
the moon shone through cloud,
you sat with your head bowed;
but now, look at the light! —

snowlight from clear blue skies
glistening where it lies,
a miraculous white varnish.
Where its drift finishes
pines in the winter wood
are green, and the streams dance.

The house gleams with radiance
and the birch-burning fire
blazes up for a new day.
Oh, we could sit and stare,
but let's get out the sleigh
and bridle the sorrel mare.

Scattering the squeaky snow
our steaming pony races
through lonely field and meadow,

forest too thickly grown
in the hot months, and down
to the river, our favourite place.

The Cloud

from the Russian of Alexander Pushkin

The storm is over and done.
A last cloud hangs alone,
the final puff of smoke
in a blue sky, its dark
shadow the last to limp
from forest, field and swamp.

Not long since the heavens burst.
When lightning split the night
and thunder rolled its drum
you were a part of that,
cloud, raining on mud-dim
provinces racked by thirst.

War and peace: the amazing,
terrible storm has gone
and earth shines in the sun
as slowly you drift away
on a leaf-relieving breeze.
There's not a cloud in the sky.

Jersey and Guernsey

from the French of Victor Hugo, 1802-1885

1

What you can see from here is chalks and ochres,
ridged furrows radiating on ploughed acres,
a stubble field half hidden by a copse
with a few hayricks here and there, the tops
of chimneys smoking up the paintable scene;
a river, not the Seine but, mixed with brine,
the thin, slow-winding local watercourse;
on the right, northwards, ugly mounds and worse
looking as if just dumped there with a spade;
a former chapel with its spire beside
a stand of crooked elms. One notices,
on looking closer, their impatient faces
scolding the north wind for its derisive
impudence. So much for the perspective.
An old cart sits and rusts next to my entrance
and there before me is a vast expanse
of deeply breathing salt water: the sea!
    A few fowl, showing off their golden finery,
gabble beneath the window, and a song
comes from a grain loft in the island tongue.
Up the lane lives an ancient ropemaker
loudly at work as the thick weave gets thicker,
the hemp twisted around his twisted loins.
Bewildering breezes blow and the sun shines:
I could walk for ever in this open space.
Book-bearing pupils envy my easy ways
in the rented schoolhouse lodgings where I stay
like a big boy on an extended holiday,
hearing for hours on end the faint murmur
of children reading aloud on the ground floor.
    A stream flows, in the fresh air a finch goes by;

so, giving thanks, I live from day to day
peacefully, in my own good time, and spend
it writing, always thinking of you, dear friend.
I listen to the young ones and, at rare
moments, watch an imposing ship stand clear
beyond the gables of the tranquil town
perhaps for a long passage, heading down
to the ocean with its wings spread, wind-driven
which last night sheltered in a quiet haven.
Neither the tears of parents, fears of wives,
the dark shadow of rocks beneath the waves
nor the gulls' agitated importunity
can hold it back from the demanding sea.

2

Sun on the eyes, clear voices, open windows,
St Peter's chimes creating quite a din.
Sea bathers shout: *No, nearer; farther. No,*
right there! Songbirds are chirping, Jenny too.
George calls her, cocks crow, and a builder's spade
scrapes somewhere. Horses pass by on the road.
Thrash of a scythe clearing a field; the gruff
mumble of men re-tiling a slate roof.
Port noises, whistle of steam-driven machinery.
Gusts of band music; cheers down at the quay.
French spoken here: *Bonjour, merci.* I'm late
rising, for (look!) here comes my favourite
robin now, cheeping at a window ledge.
Uproar of hammers from a distant forge.
Waves flap, and a steamer wheezes breezily;
enter a fly, the vast breath of the sea.

THE CHIMERAS

El Desdichado

from the French of Gérard de Nerval, 1808-1855

I am the widower — dim, disconsolate —
the Aquitainian prince in the ruined tower; my only
star is dead, my constellated lute
emblazoned with the black *sun* of *Melancholy.*

To the dark tomb, you who assuaged my hurt,
bring Posilippo and the Tyrrhenian Sea,
the *flower* that comforted my desolate heart
and the vine leaves of the rose-wreathed balcony.

I am what childe of legend or romance?
My brow burns with a queenly kiss; my dreams
have visited the cave where the Siren swims.

I've crossed the Styx in triumph twice, my hands
tuning the Orphean lyre alternately
to the saint's rapture and the fairy's cry.

Myrtho

from the French of Gérard de Nerval

Myrtho, dark sorceress, I think of you;
of noble Posilippo — dome of fire —
your features sculpted to an orient glow,
the black grapes clustered in your golden hair.

Yours was the cup where I had drunk the light
of secret lore, and yours the smiling face
the night I fell at Dionysus' feet,
Muse-naturalized among the sons of Greece.

Why the volcano stirred again I know:
your light feet flitted there. Abruptly, clouds
of cindery black smoke obscured the sun.

A Norman duke shattered your earthen gods —
since when, beneath the Virgilian laurel bough,
hydrangea and the green myrtle grow as one.

Horus

from the French of Gérard de Nerval

Shaking, the god Kneph shook the galaxies.
Isis, the mother, leaned on a bedpost
and stared at her fierce husband with disgust;
an ancient fervour gleamed in her green eyes.

'Look!' she exclaimed, 'he's dying, the old fraud!
He's drunk the hoar-frosts of the earth. Put out
his bad eye, and tie up his twisted foot —
a wintry king and a volcanic god.

'A new voice speaks to me, the eagle gone.
I have put on, for him, Cybele's gown —
for him, for Hermes' and Osiris' son!'

The goddess on her gold conch disappeared;
the sea gave back the face that we adored.
The heavens, clothed in Iris' rainbow, shone.

Anteros

from the French of Gérard de Nerval

You ask me why I have a heart made mad
and, on a snake's neck, a defiant face?
Sprung as I am from old Antaeus' race,
I fling the spears back at the conquering god.

Yes, I am one of those Revenge inspires
that kissed my forehead with its ulcerous mouth.
I've felt the furious flush of Cain beneath
my murdered brother's blood-commingled tears.

The last subdued by your superior power,
Jehovah, screaming 'Tyrant!' from the pit,
was Baal or Dagon, father or ancestor.

Thrice they immersed me in Cocytus. Now,
sole tutelary, the dragon teeth I sow
before my expropriated mother's feet.

Delphica

from the French of Gérard de Nerval

Beneath the sycamore, the shining laurel,
the olive, myrtle, or frail willow tree,
Daphne, do you recall that ancient tale,
that love song which begins continually?

The Temple with the enormous colonnade,
the lemons harsh upon the tongue — remember? —
and that dark chasm, death to the hasty, where
the cold seed of the slain dragon is laid?

They will come back, the archaic gods you mourn!
Time will restore the frame of ancient days.
Earth shivers with a prophetic undertone . . .

Meanwhile the sibyl with the Roman face
slumbers beneath the Arch of Constantine,
which stands unmoved in its appointed place.

Artemis

from the French of Gérard de Nerval

Thirteen o'clock, and the first hour once more —
always the only hour, the only minute.
Diana, are you finite or infinite?
Was I your only or your final lover?

The goddess carved on the provincial clock
of childhood loves you as she always did.
Return that love for its delight and dread.
The *Rose* she holds is the frail hollyhock.

O Neapolitan saint with hands of fire,
rose with the violet heart, St. Gudula's flower,
did you find crucifixion in the bare skies?

You who affront our gods, white roses, wither!
Disperse, pale phantoms, from your burning ether!
The saint of the void is holier to my eyes.

Gethsemane

from the French of Gérard de Nerval

God is dead; the heavens are empty . . .
Weep, children, you have no father now!

— Jean-Paul Richter

I

When the Lord, raising to heaven his wasted hands
within the sacred grove, as poets do,
abstracted in his silent sorrow, knew
himself abandoned by his faithless friends,

he turned to those still sleeping there, each head
sunk in its dream of thrones and prophecies
— but stupidly, as in a brute repose —
and lifted up his voice: 'There is no God!'

They slept. 'My friends, know the *new thing*, my brow
has touched the great vault of eternity;
I've been in agony for so long now

'and I deceived you. Darkness! God is gone
from the altar stone where I, the scapegoat, lie . . .
There is no God, no God!' But they slept on.

2

'All is dead,' he continued. 'I who've scoured
the heavens, and faltered in their starry lanes
— wherever life, of its abundant hoard,
scatters its beaches and its blue lagoons —

'found breakers crashing on deserted shores,
a confused throng of agitated seas . . .
A vague breath motivates the vagrant spheres
but there is no life in the galaxies.

'Striving to catch the eye of God, I faced
an empty socket beaming its black night
over the world with ever-thickening rays.

'An unexpected rainbow rings that pit —
threshold of chaos and the dark, a vast
whirlpool swallowing up the Worlds and Days!'

3

'Unmoving Destiny, mute sentry, grim
Necessity — as you meander through
the dead worlds shrouded in eternal snow
slowly freezing the universe — O prime

'mover, can you be sure what you're about
with extinct suns bouncing around in space?
Are you convinced the vital breath will pass
to a reborn world from a world burnt out?

'Is this your presence in me, father? Have
you power to live and power to cheat the grave?
Or will you yield before one final heave

'of the anathematized night angel? I
am alone here with my fear and misery,
and if I die then everything must die!'

4

Nobody heard the eternal victim cry
as he poured out his heart in vain to them.
Now, broken, on the point of fainting, he
called to the *one* wakeful in Jerusalem.

'Judas!' he shouted, 'you know what I'm worth.
Betray me quick, old friend, and get it done.
I am in agony, stretched out on the earth;
you have at least the vitality of your sin.'

Judas had left, though, racked by shame and guilt —
resentful too, thinking himself ill-paid.
He read his treachery on every brick.

Pilate alone, the eyes of Caesar, felt
a twinge of pity, pondered, turned and said
to his subordinates: 'Fetch this lunatic.'

5

This lunatic was Icarus who, though wrecked,
reclimbed the heavens; Phaeton obscured again
by thunder-darkened skies; and Atys slain
whom once a year Cybele resurrects.

They probed the entrails of the sacrifice,
earth drowned its sorrow in the haemorrhage;
Olympus tottered briefly towards the abyss,
the night sky shook in its revolving cage.

'Who is this new god foisted on the earth?'
Caesar demanded of great Jupiter,
'Is he a deity or a fiend? Reply!'

But the oracle was dumb from that day forth.
One only could resolve the mystery —
whoever breathed life into the primal mire.

Pythagorean Lines

from the French of Gérard de Nerval

— *Everything feels!*

Man, do you think yourself the one reflective
thing in this lively world? Your urgent guile
works blithely on its raw material,
but you ignore the spiritual perspective.

Respect the dog's life and the worm's-eye view;
each flower in nature is an open soul.
Love lives even in the zinc of a zinc bowl:
everything feels, and leaves its mark on you.

Note, in the wall, a fierce interrogation.
Dumb matter is the word made flesh, therefore
subject it to no base manipulation.

Even now a god hides among bricks and bones —
and, like an eye closed in the womb, a pure
spirit evolves beneath the glaze of stones!

Antrim Road

from the French of Charles Baudelaire, 1821-1867

I can still see that first suburban house,
whitewashed and tiny, tiny but at peace,
a 'Dresden' figurine next to the clock
holding her skirt out as she reads a book.
A fiery evening sun, intensely hot,
burns at the window from a garden hut,
a curious red eye between two clouds
silently watching mushy peas and spuds,
and throws out long, imposing shadow shapes
on the white homework and the bottled ships.

Scene

from the French of Charles Baudelaire

Blithely to draft these scribbles I need to lie,
like the astrologers, in an attic next the sky
where, high among church spires, I can dream and hear
their grave hymns wind-blown to my ivory tower.
Chin in hand, up here in my apartment block,
I can see workshops full of noise and talk,
cranes and masts of the ocean-going city,
vast cloud-lit photographs of eternity.
I watch a foggy star open and shine
in the azure sky, a lamp at a windowpane,
smoke rising into the firmament like incense,
the moon dispensing its mysterious influence.
I watch for spring and summer, autumn too;
and when the winter comes, with silent snow,
I shut the shutters and close the curtains tight
to build my faerie palaces in the night
and think of love and gardens, blue resorts,
white fountains splashing into marble courts,
birds chirping day and night, whatever notion
tickles the infantile imagination . . .
Rattling the window with its hoarse burlesque
no mob distracts me from my writing desk;
for here I am, up to my usual tricks —
evoking springtime on the least pretext,
extracting sunlight as my whims require,
my thoughts blazing for want of a real fire.

Dusk

from the French of Charles Baudelaire

Night now, bewitching night, friend of the evil-doer,
sneaks up like an accomplice; like a boudoir
the sky closes; and men, mild in themselves,
change into ravening vampires and werewolves.
Soft night, desired by the unfortunate ones
whose limbs articulate with aches and groans
a day of servitude; night that relieves
those victims sacrificed to arduous lives —
the driven thinker with his ashen face,
the cleaning woman who can know release.
Unwholesome spirits in the atmosphere
wake stupidly, meanwhile, like businessmen
and, cruising bat-like through the evening air,
flap at the doorpost and the windowpane.
Under the lamplight that the wind teases
the whores light up outside the whorehouses
like ants pouring out of their black holes;
insurgents waiting for the word to strike,
they fan out everywhere through dark defiles
in diseased organs of the body politic
like flies that buzz around an open sewer.
You can hear a kitchen whistle here and there,
a playhouse laugh, a concert thump and blare;
the new rich, loud with brandy and cigars,
fill up the restaurants and cocktail bars
while thieves with neither pity nor remorse
will soon be at their dirty work, of course,
rifling the strongbox and the bureau drawers
to stuff their face and clothe their paramours.
Be still, my soul, at this unearthly hour
and stop your ears to its incessant roar,
for now the sufferings of the sick increase.
Night takes them by the throat, their struggles cease

as one by one they head for the great gulf;
the wards fill with their cries, who soon enough
will come no more to sup the fragrant broth
with a loved one, at dusk, by a known hearth —
for some of us have never known the relief
of house and home, being outcast in this life.

Afternoon Sex

from the French of Charles Baudelaire

Although your wicked brows
give you a strange look
so far from angelic,
witch with enticing eyes

frivolous and skittish,
I love you in slow motion
with the fierce adoration
of a priest for his fetish.

Desert and forest scent
the thick, swinging hair
you shake out with an air
mysterious and intent.

Nymph tenebrous and warm,
your wild limbs dispense
an odour like incense
rich with a vespral charm.

No potion, however strong,
equals the given head
when you raise the dead
under your cunning tongue.

Delirious with self-hunger
for your own breasts and back,
you ravish the hot sack
in a delicious languor.

At times, as if to subdue
some peculiar spite,

you concentrate on the bite
and on the serious screw,

tearing at hip and thigh
with a primeval giggle;
and then my frantic goggle
rests in your lunar eye.

Beneath your satin heel
and silken toe I set
my genius, my delight,
my fate and my dark soul —

a soul given new light
and colour by this bright
explosion of white heat
in my Siberian night!

The Lady from the Sea

from the Norwegian of Henrik Ibsen, 1828-1906

She Born in a lighthouse, I still find it hard
as wife to a doctor ten miles from the coast.
My home is a pleasant one but I get bored;
the mountains bother me. Now, like a ghost,
you show up here, severe and adamant.
What are you anyhow? What do you want?

He I am a simple man upon the land,
I am a seal upon the open sea.
Your eyes are of the depths. Give me your hand,
give me your heart and come away with me
to the Spice Islands, the South Seas; anywhere.
Only the force of habit keeps you here.

She Even up here, enclosed, I sniff the brine,
the open sea out there beyond the beach;
my thoughts are waves, my dreams are estuarine
and deeper than an anchor chain could reach.
I knew you'd come, like some demonic fate
glimpsed at a window or a garden gate.

He How can you live here with no real horizon,
someone like you, a mermaid and a Muse,
a figment of your own imagination,
the years elapsing like a tedious cruise?
Your settled life is like this summer glow;
dark clouds foreshadow the approaching snow.

She Sometimes, emerging from my daily swim
or gazing from the dock these quiet nights,
I know my siren soul; and in a dream
I stare astonished at the harbour lights,

hugging my knees and sitting up alone
as ships glide darkly past with a low moan.

He If our mad race had never left the sea,
had we remained content with mud and rock,
we might have saved ourselves great misery;
though even this evening we could still go back.
Think of the crashing breakers, the dim haze
of a salt sun rising on watery days.

She My wild spirit unbroken, should I return
to the tide, choosing at last my other life,
reverting to blue water and sea-brine,
or do I continue as a faithful wife?
If faithful is the word for one who clings
to the lost pre-existence of previous things.

He Do you remember the great vow you made
to the one man you chose from other men?
The years have come between, with nothing said,
and now the stranger has appeared again
to claim your former love and make it new.
You ask me what I am; but what are you?

She I am a troubled woman on the land,
I am a seal upon the open sea,
but it's too late to give my heart and hand
to someone who remains a mystery.
Siren or not, this is my proper place;
go to your ship and leave me here in peace.

Art poétique

from the French of Paul Verlaine, 1844-1896

The music is the important thing.
Opt for the odd, the singular,
the faint, the soluble in air,
no rhetoric and no posturing.

Take note, it's absolutely fine
to sound a bit ambiguous;
best is a grey, indefinite verse
where the exact and vague combine —

behind the veil a twinkling eye,
vibration of the noonday light,
a violet star concourse, bright
in an exhausted autumn sky.

Not primary colour but nuance,
nuance alone that can unite
dream to dream and horn to flute,
informs all such experience.

Resist the lure of biting 'wit',
the glib reductionism, the cheap
sarcasm at which angels weep.
Avoid the nasty taste of it.

Take eloquence and wring its neck
and, while we're at it, it's high time
to be more circumspect with rhyme.
If not, it soon dictates the work.

The damage it has done already!
What daft idiot, deaf to tone,

forged from tin this specious coin
that rings so thin to everybody?

Music and yet more music, please!
May your own song be something light
we hear soaring, a soul in flight
to other loves and other skies.

May it presage the greater future
borne on a brisk morning wind
bestowing scents of thyme and mint.
The rest is only literature.

Down in the Woods

from the French of Paul Verlaine

Some, like the innocent and the neurasthenic,
find in the woods only a languorous charm,
fresh breezes, warm scents. Good luck to them.
Others, dreamers, are seized with vague panic.

Good luck to them! I, nervous and aghast,
racked by a strange, insistent guilt complex,
tremble here like a faintheart who expects
a trap, perhaps an encounter with a ghost.

These great boughs, like sea waves never still,
with their dark silences and even darker
shadows — a sad and sinister décor —
inspire fears both profound and risible.

Worst is summer dusk when a fiery sky
merges in the grey-blue of mists its range
of blood hues while a distant Angelus
rings out like the echo of a plaintive cry.

Wind rises hot, strong; wild convulsions race
crazily through the increasingly opaque
density of the oaks until, grown weak,
they escape like exhalations into space.

Night hovers, an owl flies, and you think back
to grim rumours warning of awful things.
Below a thicket there, *there*, hidden springs
chuckle like killers lying in wait to strike.

Old Roscoff

from the French of Tristan Corbière, 1845-1875

Bolt-hole of brigandage, old keep
of piracy, the ocean booms
on membranes of your granite sleep
and thunders in your brackish dreams.
Snore the sea and snore the sky,
snore the foghorn in your ears;
sleep with your one watchful eye
on England these three hundred years.

Sleep, old hulk for ever anchored
where the wild goose and cormorant,
your elegists, cry to the barred
and salt-laced shutters on the front.
Sleep, old whore of the homing seamen
heady with wind and wine; no more
will hot gold subdue your women
as a spring tide engulfs your shore.

Sleep in the dunes beneath the grey
gunmetal clouds; the pennants gone,
no grapeshot now will ricochet
or drum rumble. Pungent dawn
will find your children dream-ensnared
by the great days when giants trod
the timbered piers and cynosured
the shopping lanes and promenade.

Your cannon, swept by wintry rain,
lie prostrate on their beds of mud.
Their mouths will never speak again;
they sleep the long sleep of the dead,

their only roar the adenoidal
echoes of equinoctial snores
from the cold muzzles pointing still
at England, trailing a few wildflowers.

Insomnia

from the French of Tristan Corbière

Insomnia, you shadowy creature,
are you a girl-in-the-head only,
you who get such a wicked kick
invigilating by the clock
the twisted pillow and night torture
under your dark and sparkling eye?

What do I call you? Hope? Regret?
Why, during the wakeful hours
rainy as Sunday, do you come
to lick our faces like a pet
and whisper in our throbbing ears
no word to break the tedium?

Why do you always offer up
to the dry throat an empty cup
and leave us with an aching brain,
tantalized, hugging fantasies?
Our love potions are bitter lees,
hot lead weighs on the dewy dawn.

You're ravishing of course — Oh, yes! —
but why the torment, why the tease?
Why squeeze us tight between your knees?
Why moan like that as if in heat,
churn up the blanket and the sheet
and never really sleep with us?

And why, grim Lady of the Night,
this black mask covering your face?
To sharpen piquancy? You come
into my own private space

like a deranged man-eater from
the old days, still not satisfied.

You're a hysterical symptom, right?
Repetitive, like the same old tune
played over and over again,
a plectrum plucking at the needy
nerves of us poor sods who write
lines that nobody else will read.

Are you Titania from the *Dream*?
The Night Mare? Or a Monster Moth?
Your fiery tongue leaves in the mouth
an icy taste of white-hot iron.
Into the bed now and lie down:
why don't we try it one more time?

from The Drunken Boat

from the French of Arthur Rimbaud, 1854-1891

As I came down the dreamy streams I knew
when the restraining towrope slackened; crazed
Apaches seized and nailed the hauling crew
naked to stakes where fiery feathers blazed.

Not that I cared: relieved of the dull weight
of cautious men and inventoried cargo
— phlegmatic flax, quotidian grain — I let
the current carry me where I chose to go.

Deaf to the furious whisperings of the sand,
my heart rose to a tidal detonation;
peninsulas, ripped screaming from the land,
crashed in a stinging mist of exultation.

Storms smiled on my salt sea-morning sleep.
I danced, light as a cork, nine nights or more
upon the intractable, skull-trundling deep,
contemptuous of the blinking lights ashore.

Juice of the oceans, tart as unripe fruit,
burst on my spruce boards in tongues of brine
that tore the spinning binnacle from its root,
rinsing the curdled puke and the blue wine;

and then I was submerged in a sea-poem
infused with milky stars, gulped the profound
viridian where, disconsolate and calm,
rapt faces drifted past of the long drowned.

I saw skies split by lightning, granite waves
shaking the earth, ambrosial dusks and dawns,

day risen aloft, a multitude of doves —
and, with a wild eye, archetypal visions;

watched horizontal orbs, like spotlights trained
on some barbaric tragedy of old,
direct their peacock rays along the sun-blind
waters, and heard their clattering slats unfold.

I dreamed the emerald snow of dazzling chasms,
kisses ascending to the eyes of the sea,
the circulation of mysterious plasms
and mornings loud with phosphorous harmony.

Trembling, I heard volcanic eructations,
a thrash of behemoths; but now, my ears
weary of this crescendo of sensations,
I thought of Europe and her ancient towers.

Delirious capes! Strewn archipelagoes!
Do you nurse there in your galactic foam
the glistening bodies of obscure flamingoes
tranced in a prescience of the life to come?

Europe of cloud canals, I would ask of you
only the pond where, on a quiet evening,
an only child launches a toy canoe
as frail and pitiful as a moth in spring.

Romance

from the French of Arthur Rimbaud

1

Nothing is serious when you're seventeen.
One evening, sick of the beer and the lemonade,
the noise and bright lights of the café scene,
you sit out under trees on the promenade.

A scent of lime there in the hot June nights.
The air engulfs you with its summery glow;
not far away the wine fumes and the shouts
float up on a soft breeze from down below.

2

You try to fix your gaze on a patch of blue
framed like a picture in the branchy night
pierced by a star, sharp but dissolving now,
quivering slightly, tiny, perfectly white.

A June night! Seventeen! You're getting drunk.
You sip champagne, the stuff goes to your head;
you wander off, imagining some punk
groupie clinging to you or in your bed.

3

The daft heart drifts to popular romance —
when, suddenly, that nice Nanette goes by,
delightful in the pale glare of the lamps
under her stuffy father's furious eye.

Since you look interesting, if a little weird,
she throws you an alert and lively glance,

two shoes tickety-boo in the boulevard,
and a soppy song dies on your lips at once.

    4

Now you're in love (she giggles at your poem) —
in love, until the holidays are through.
Your pals avoid you, love being 'bad form',
and the next day she grants a rendezvous . . . !

That evening, back to the rowdy café scene,
ordering up the beer and the lemonade.
Nothing is serious when you're seventeen
and lime trees are in leaf on the promenade.

The Cupboard

from the French of Arthur Rimbaud

Unlock this great old cupboard of carved oak
and it gives out intriguing intimations
like a wine bin chock-full of vintage wines;
the wood has the fine grain of ancient folk.

It's packed with a jumble of inherited stuff —
clean yellow linen, the limp withered laces
of aunts and children, period bits and pieces,
moth-eaten granny scarves adorned with griffins.

Here are the lockets, the locks blonde and white
of faded hair, the portraits, the dried violets
whose scent is mingled with the scents of fruit.

Old cupboard, what strange truths you could reveal!
I know you're desperate to tell your secrets:
as the dark doors swing open you slowly squeal.

The Hitch Hiker

from the French of Arthur Rimbaud

Beneath an open sky, the Muses' boy,
off I would go, one fist in a torn pocket
of my virtual, ghost-of-a-jacket donkey jacket,
picturing the great adventures I'd enjoy.

Roaming under the heavens I scattered pearls
of poetry, a rock star in my dreams.
There was an old rip in my filthy jeans;
lights danced on the sky like chorus girls.

Crashing at night in fields and outbuildings
I'd versify among fantastic shadows,
skin dew-anointed for the sake of art;

I'd pluck at the broken lyre of my shoestrings
and listen to the mild September meadows,
one ruined sneaker close to my hungry heart.

The Travel Section

from the French of Jules Laforgue, 1860-1887

I'm reading about life on the prairie and frontier
when a voice cries: 'Hey, you could live here!'
Outcast from the old world, a desperado
without God or government, where could I not go?
Out there I'll scalp my European brain,
run wild like a young colt on the open plain —
a sort of post-literate, Huck Finn child of nature
or existential citizen of the future,
an idealistic rustic, rancher, architect,
hunter, fisherman, gambler, prickly autodidact;
and live, buckskin-clad, on whiskey and pot-roast
between Colorado and the Pacific Coast,
sleeping out under pre-Columbian skies
more generous than our bourgeois certainties!
And? A mystique of campsites, the Lynch law,
rough diamonds to clutch in my grubby paw,
a gold rush over the desert at first light,
a poker school around the fire at night.
When I grow old, a farm in the sunrise,
a dairy cow, grandchildren at my knees
and, slung from the twin cow-horns over the gate,
a split-pine signboard advertising 'Body Art';
and if fond memories of the rue de Seine
tempt me with thoughts of coming home again
I'll start a new cult based on holistic books,
blithe and post-modern, for the post-pastoral folks.

Sunday

from the French of Jules Laforgue

Rain pours down without purpose or reason
on wood and meadow, on the faint horizon.
The river too is having a Sunday snooze,
no barges heading either upstream or down,
no *fêtes champêtres* on its deserted shores.
Angelus bells are ringing round the town,
church-going schoolgirls shivering in their shoes.
Twilight, and stormy harbour lights come on
arranged in a familiar *mise-en-scène*.
Autumn winds are back now with a vengeance,
curtains closed for the annual winter break.
I've spent my whole life failing to make changes
and thinking about the trains I didn't take.
Young woman, first floor, practising the piano,
run off with me into the night, let's go
native on this the only earth we have
which houses us in the end no matter what,
ignore celestial will-o'-the-wisps and love
the glow-worms of our own terrestrial state:
even with catarrh, life isn't really desperate
so long as we don't expect too much of it.
Autumn, dead leaves blocking up the drain;
repetitive pop music, harsh, inane,
maddening . . . C'mon, last of the poets: hide
indoors, you commit gradual suicide —
and look, the rain's stopped, everyone's outside!
Why don't you go get something for your flu,
that will be a nice little walk for you.

Complaint of the Organist of Notre Dame de Nice

from the French of Jules Laforgue

Tonight a wintry crow extrudes
its croaky psalm from the bell-tower;
and now, here comes an autumn shower.
Goodbye to the casino woods!

She looked even ghastlier today,
her whole frame shivering, cold and blue.
(This empty church is icy too.)
Nobody loves her now but me.

I'd gladly cut my heart out, wild
for one smile from her mournful mien,
faithful to whom I shall remain
down here in the triumphant world.

The hour she quits this earthly sphere
I mean to play a *Miserere*
cosmic in its rich despair
so God himself will surely hear!

I'll sit here in the growing darkness
true to my dead phthisic lover,
rocking my broken heart for ever
to the eternal fugues of Bach.

Each year, the same day as her death,
devoted to her as I am,
I shall unchain this *Requiem*
I've written for the death of Earth.

from ALEXANDRIA

from the Greek of Constantine Cavafy, 1863-1933

The Souls of the Old Men

The souls of the old men
cling to their bodies
with fierce loyalty, with love
born of necessity:
where else could they live?

Gazing from behind clouded eyes
they are tired
of the old habitations,
resentful of their own
impatience to be gone.

The Life We Know

I will not be known by what I did or said.
The facts of life conspired
to block action, tie tongue; nothing
came out as I intended.

No, look for my secret
in the lost grin,
the poker-faced elision.

Reborn in the ideal society
I shall act and speak
with a freedom denied me
by the life we know.

The Enchanted Wood

from the French of Paul Valéry, 1871-1945

Amid rustling leaves and leaf shadows her moist
breath rises and falls in the silent hall;
magpies alight beside her glittering wrist,
her lips almost compose one coral vowel.
She listens neither to the quiet raindrops
tinkling the coin of the submerged decades
nor to the flute wind in the dreaming copse
where the horn note of a distant hunt subsides.

To these dwindling echoes she faintly sighs,
grown indistinct among the dark bushes
waving and tapping at her buried ear;
and the slow rose whispering to her eyes
never disturbs the hotly rumpled creases
secretly conscious of the sunlight there.

The Seaside Cemetery

from the French of Paul Valéry

A tranquil surface where a spinnaker moves
flickers among the pines, among the graves;
objective noon films with its fiery glaze
a shifting sea, drifters like dipping doves,
and my reward for thought is a long gaze
down the blue calm of these celestial groves.

When, as now, light freezes above the gulf,
a gem revolving in its radiant gleam
such many-faceted and glittering foam
that a great peace seems to extend itself,
those clear-cut artifacts of the continuum,
time and knowledge, take the shape of a dream.

Wide-open vault and chaste shrine to Athene,
deep reservoir of calmly shining money,
like an eye the supercilious water structure
lies somnolent beneath its burning veils;
and my soul silence too is architecture,
a golden hoard roofed with a thousand tiles.

Temple of time I breathe when I breathe in,
to this high point I climb and feel at home
ordering all things with a seaward stare
of circumspection; and, as my supreme
offering to the gods, the serene glare
sows on the depths an imperious disdain.

But even as fruit consumes itself in taste,
even as it translates its own demise
deliciously in the mouth where its form dies,
I sniff already my own future smoke

while light sings to the ashen soul the quick
change starting now on the murmuring coast.

Under this clear sky it is I who change —
after so much conceit, after such strange
idleness, but bursting with new power,
I give myself up to these brilliant spaces;
on the mansions of the dead my shadow passes
reminding me of its own ephemeral hour.

A soul-exposure to the solar torches
I can endure, and the condign tortures
of the midsummer's pitiless bronze light;
and though submission show a midnight face
invisible in daytime, to that bright
presence I concede the superior place.

Stopped at a cistern with a pumping heart
between the vacuum and the creative act
whispering to my preliminary tact,
I await the echo of an interior force,
that bitter, dark and sonorous water source
ringing in depths beyond the reach of art.

Caged though you seem behind a mesh of branches,
great gulf, consumer of these meagre fences,
a blinding secret on the lids, reveal
what body draws me to its indolences,
what face invites me to this bony soil.
A faint spark ponders these inheritances.

Composed of sombre trees, of light and stone,
an earthly splinter held up to the sun,
sacred, enclosed in immaterial fire,

I like this place with its dark poplar flames,
the marble glimmering in the shadows here
where a faithful sea snores on the table tombs.

And if, sole shepherd, with a pastoral eye
I gaze too long on these mysterious flocks,
on these white souls, each in its tranquil box,
may the sea's growl dispel the idolatrous things,
frightening off the prudent doves, the coy
illusions and the angels' curious wings.

The future, here already, scarcely moves.
A quick insect scratches the dry leaves;
everything is exhausted, scorched by the air
into I don't know what rigorous form.
Dazed with diversity, the enormous swarm
of life is bitter-sweet and the mind clear.

The hidden dead lie easy in this soil
which holds them tight and seasons their mystique;
high up the southern noon, completely still,
reflects upon itself where none may look.
Absolute monarch, firmament of blue,
I am the secret difference now in you.

I am the one your worst fears validate —
my cowardice, my bad thoughts, my contrition
make up the one flaw in your precious opal;
and meanwhile, in a dense marmoreal night
among the roots, vague oceanic people
have long ago arrived at your conclusion.

Mixed in a thick solution underground
the white clay is drunk by the crimson kind;
its vigour circulates in the veined flowers.

Where now are the colloquial turns of phrase,
the individual gifts and singular souls?
Where once a tear gathered a grub crawls.

The ticklish virgins with their twittering cries,
the teeth, the eyelids and the gentle eyes,
enchanted breasts heaving in provocation,
glistening lips shiny with invitation,
the last delights, the fingers that resist,
all join the circle and return to dust.

And you, great soul, dare you hypostasize
a world untarnished by the luminous lies
the sun and sea suggest to mortal eyes?
Will you still sing when you've become a ghost?
Nonsense, everything flows, ourselves the most;
the hunger for eternity also dies.

Gaunt immortality, gold carved on black,
cold consolation crowned with a laurel wreath
that makes a maternal bosom of grim death,
a gorgeous fiction and a lugubrious joke —
who doesn't know, and who would not decline
the empty skull with its eternal grin?

Archaic progenitors, your derelict heads
returned to pasture by so many spades,
no longer knowing the familiar tread —
the real ravager, the irrefutable worm
is not for you, at peace now in the tomb;
it lives on life and never leaves my side.

Self-love, self-hatred, what's the difference?
Its secret mordancy is so intense
the silent gnawing goes by many names.

Watching, desiring, nibbling, considering,
it likes the flesh and, even in my dreams,
I live on sufferance of this ravenous thing.

Zeno, harsh theorist of conceptual zero,
have you transfixed me with your winged arrow
which quivers, flies, yet never leaves the bow?
These paradoxes strike me from the shade.
Am I afraid now of my own shadow,
the mighty hero frozen in mid-stride?

No, no; get up, go on to the next phase —
body, shake off this meditative pose
and, chest, inhale the first flap of the air.
A palpable new freshness off the sea,
an ozone rush, restores my soul to me
and draws me down to the reviving shore.

Great sea endowed with frenzy and sensation,
slick panther-hide and heaving vegetation
sown with a million images of the sun;
unchained monster drunk on your blue skin,
chewing for ever your own glistening tail
in a perpetual, silent-seeming turmoil,

the wind rises; it's time to start. A vast breeze
opens and shuts the notebook on my knees.
Uproarious waves explode among the rocks
flashing; fly off, then, my sun-dazzled pages
and break, waves, break up with ecstatic surges
this shifting surface where the spinnaker flocks!

Villonelle

from the French of Max Jacob, 1874-1944

The Sirens — tell me, what bewitching
song did they sing so many a butch
hero would stare from his trireme
as it approached the fatal cliff
and ship his oar to live the dream?

The thug who captured Troy — a spiteful
adversary, hard-hearted, tough —
was once held captive by a gang
of singing virgins. Aphrodite,
what was the song the virgins sang?

Náusicaa at her washing, grave
Penelope at her weaving, wove
their *own* melodious sentiments.
Oh, dwindling echoes, long laments,
the mournful songs of emigrants . . . !

Where are the songs we liked to sing
in the old days? Dispersed and gone,
like the young ones we used to love
who sang to keep love flourishing.
And I, will I forget my own?

Jardin du Luxembourg

from the German of Rainer Maria Rilke, 1875-1926

A merry-go-round of freshly painted horses
sprung from a childish world vividly bright
before dispersing in adult oblivion
and losing its quaint legendary light
spins in the shadows of a burbling circus.
Some draw toy coaches but remain upright;
a roebuck flashes past, a fierce red lion
and every time an elephant ivory-white.

As if down in the forest of Fontainebleau
a little girl wrapped up in royal blue
rides round on a unicorn; a valiant son
hangs on to the lion with a frantic laugh,
hot fists gripping the handles for dear life;
then that white elephant with ivory tusks —
an intense scrum of scarves and rumpled socks
though the great whirligig is just for fun.

The ring revolves until the time runs out,
squealing excitedly to the final shout
as pop-eyed children gasp there in their grey
jackets and skirts, wild bobble and beret.
Now you can study faces, different types,
the tiny features starting to take shape
with proud, heroic grins for the grown-ups,
shining and blind as if from a mad scrape.

Night Drive

from the German of Rainer Maria Rilke

— *St. Petersburg, 1900*

Not drawn but flown by glistening mares
past silent, tomb-lit porticoes
and lamp-posts hung like chandeliers,
past granite palaces where a first
dawn-glow lightened the roofs, we burst
on to the windy Neva quays,
rumbling there in an anxious, thin
half-light neither of earth nor heaven,
leaving behind the unwoken, dark
woods of the Czar's private park
protected from the risen breeze,
its statues fading, every gest-
ure frozen for ever in the past.
St. Petersburg ceased to exist,
disclosed that it had never been;
asked only peace now, as if one
long mad should find the knot untied
and watch, recovered and clear-eyed,
a fixed idea in its Byzantine,
varnished and adamantine shrine
spin off from the whirling mind
and vanish, leaving not a trace behind.

Borgeby-Gard

from the German of Rainer Maria Rilke

Two paths diverge in a favourite northern park.
You hesitate, step out with renewed vigour,
go down the mistier, more mysterious one
and for a minute or two you're in the dark;
but you come to a clearing and a mouldy stone
inscribed to the memory of Sophie Brigge.
She pours like powder from your crumbling fist:
why does she rouse this never-failing interest?

What is it about this place that you explore
damp glades the other visitors ignore?
While you malinger at the sunlit rose
what are you listening for, what distant voices?
Why do you watch with such bewildered eyes
the butterflies around the buddleia bushes?

Night Watch

from the German of Rainer Maria Rilke

You'd often stand at a window new to you that day
and gaze at the shadows while a strange *quartier*
closed you out with its cold architecture
as if you weren't there, and the mute furniture
paid no attention to your ignorant stare.
A pavement rose incuriously to the lamplight.
Behind open shutters, a warm family flat:
you'd watch, they'd notice you, the shutters shut.
You'd wait while a child cried, once more aware
of the tough maternity here and everywhere
and the inconsolable crying behind all life.
A drunk holds forth or a lost soul gives tongue,
a voice tries out some trite, seductive air
('the peculiar potency of popular song')
and an old man coughs insistently as if
his body still rejects the thought of death
while a clock strikes and you lose count of time
like an odd child who hasn't grasped the game;
but then you realize the great grown-up night
is watching over you and you're at peace.
As you stand, vaguely conscious of hostility,
late business growls in the mysterious city
of brisk asperities and unceasing work;
but, night descending with its infinite breath
like an open window in a country house,
you smile and take your part in the dreaming dark.

Simulacrum

from the German of Rainer Maria Rilke

Technology threatens our inherited riches —
unmindful, makes its *own* mind up and, brusque,
brushing aside the slow work of the ages,
re-shapes our materials for a colder task.

Not just a new fad we can ignore, something
in far-off factories decently wrapped in grease,
now it is life itself, 'as if', a simulacrum
torn down and redeveloped with equal ease.

Even so, existence remains magical, Orphean,
sprung from so many sources, a pure flux
striking the watchful eye with epiphanies.

Words still escape from our too quick embrace
and music, dropping in stone notes, still erects
its heavenly house in unexploitable space.

Ariel to Prospero

from the German of Rainer Maria Rilke

Deposed magician, tricked of your worldly throne,
you kept this spirit to keep an eye on you,
knowing in due course you would let me go —
but, strict in daylight, ruminative at night,
you made up reasons to postpone my flight.
My servitude, as you know, implies your own:
think of the music if our bonds were gone,
a new earth music previously unknown
even in this noisy island; think how brave
to waive your art, vacate your vatic cave
and live in the real world, breathing the air
blown to us daily in our exile here.
I flit and whistle at your slightest whim,
bored but amused by this strange interim,
and smile to think of the odd things I know:
mysterious defiles where wildflowers grow,
the secret places where new species thrive;
I've a light workload, scope for initiative . . .
Be frank, will you shed a tear when it is time?

('The cloud-capp'd towers, the gorgeous palaces'
leave not a rack behind; we hide our faces
and listen patiently as the restored duke,
doubtful about the future, drowns his book
with a few lines noted for calm restraint,
reliant on his own strength 'which is most faint'.)

from The Ill-Loved

from the French of Guillaume Apollinaire, 1880-1918

> *I put this song together when*
> *She left me inconsolable not*
> *Knowing love is like the fine*
> *Phoenix if it die one night*
> *The morning sees it born again*

One foggy day in London town
An urchin looking much the same
As my beloved came strolling by
And at the glance he threw my way
I lowered my own eyes for shame

I followed the delinquent boy
Who sauntered whistling nonchalantly
Down redbrick residential streets
The rival tides of the Red Sea
Parting for the Israelites

May these brick waves collapse if she
Was not my only well-beloved
I am the king of Egypt me
His bowmen and his sister-wife
If she was not my only life

At a bright corner shining with
Window displays like weeping wounds
In fog where fairy lights bemoaned
The retail world of shop and shelf
A woman not unlike herself

And with the same distracted gaze
The same scar on her naked neck

Emerged tight from a public house
At the same time I realized
That love itself is treacherous

When wise Odysseus got back
Finally to his own island home
His ancient hound remembered him
And weaving still at her high loom
His wife awaited the event

The husband of Sakōntala
Weary of conquering gave praise
To find her once again though pale
From anxious waiting doleful days
Fondling her much-loved gazelle

I think about their happy fate
When unrequited love and she
To whom I am devoted still
Inconstant phantoms violently
Converging make me miserable

Hell is composed of such regret
Oblivious heaven open wide
Before me princes would have died
Poor famous divils for her kiss
Or sold their very souls for this

I spent my winter in the past
Come back to us you Easter sun
Warm up the frozen heart at last
With your hot rays bring some relief
Into my disenchanted life

O memory my splendid barque
Have we not sailed too long in rough
Seas bitter brine a dismal scene
Have we not wandered far enough
From lively dawn to pensive dark

Goodbye my love I wish in vain
Since she is emigrating Annie
She who was really lost to me
L'année dernière in Germany
Whom I shall never see again . . .

. . . The sun of June an Orphic lyre
Scorches my aching knuckles hard
Plangent delirium where I
Wander into a boulevard
Too much in love with it to die

Sundays go on for ever now
A hurdy-gurdy gurgles in
The shadows of a grey courtyard
While on a balcony wan flowers
Dangle aslant like leaning towers

Parisian evenings soaked in gin
And blazing with electric light
Tram trolleys flashing emerald fire
And singing until out of sight
The crazy world of the machine

Cafés choking with nicotine
And loud with the sad gipsy tongue
The sniffling soda siphons tired
Laconic waiters all complain
To you you whom I once adored

I who know royal dirges boring
Plaints from my adolescent years
Spirituals of the tropics long
Stories of ill-love and tears
And secret songs the Sirens sang

A Siren

from the Italian of Umberto Saba, 1883-1957

Anyone watching you in the water would think: 'A siren!'
Winner in the women's swimming event, you seem
strange on the screen of my inglorious life.
While you smile in triumph I tie a thread,
a thin unbreakable thing, to your toe
but you stride past without noticing me.
Your friends, young like yourself, crowd round
and make a noise in the bar; and then
just for a moment cloud shadow, a grave
motherly shadow, shivers down
from your eyebrows to the proud, beautiful chin —

and joins your rising to my own setting sun.

White Night

from the Russian of Boris Pasternak, 1890-1960

In the distant past I can see
a house on a Petersburg quay,
your first flat, where you,
a daughter of the steppe,
had come from Kursk to be
a student and fall in love.

One white night we sat late
at your window, gazing out
at the city stretching away
beyond the endless Neva,
gas flames flickering
like moths in the street lamps.

That spring-white night we spoke
tentatively, constrained
by mysteries while, far off
in the countryside, nightingales
thronged the thick forests
with the thunder of their song.

The singing went on and on,
the birds' tiny voices
exciting a spring fever
deep in enchanted woods;
and there the dawn wind bore
the sound of our own words.

Orchards were in flower
as far as the eye could reach,
and ghostly birches crowded

into the roads as though
to wave goodbye to the white
night which had seen so much.

The Earth

from the Russian of Boris Pasternak

Spring bursts in the houses
of Moscow. A moth quits
its hiding place and flits
into the light of day
to gasp on cotton blouses;
fur coats are locked away.

The ivy shakes itself
and stretches in its pot;
attic and dusty shelf
inhale the open air.
This is the time for twilit
trysts beside the river,

time for the injudicious
out-in-the-open voices
and gossip like thaw water
dripping from the eaves;
sob stories and laughter
dance in the woken leaves.

Outside and in, the same
mixture of fire and fear,
the same delirium
of apple blossom at
window and garden gate,
tram stop and factory door.

So why does the dim horizon
weep, and the dark mould
resist? It is my chosen
task, surely, to nurse

the distances from cold,
the earth from loneliness.

Which is why, in the spring,
our friends come together
and the vodka and talking
are ceremonies, that the river
of suffering may release
the heart-constraining ice.

A Window

from the Spanish of Jorge Guillén, 1893-1984

The sky dreams cloud for the real world
whose substance is in love with space
and light. Today I noticed a sandy reef,
its dunes like ocean waves or snowdrifts:
so much racy chaos, so much caprice
teasing the eye with its irresistibly
genial reality. Here I live, at the edge
of these solid, profound transparencies.
A shifting wind encircles, defines, enhances
a branch on a tree, leaves on the branch,
gates and gardens, corners and balustrades,
serene facts of the existential evening
asking only the calm gaze of a window.
Everything in tune with its circumstances,
bright pebbles, a fence here, there a wire,
each minute shines with a crystal glow.
I'm like the glass myself, admiring the air,
its clarity so much in accordance
with sun and mind! I've polished words
but I want to know as the June air knows.
A rustling poplar makes a visible breeze,
the twilight describes a circle of peace
and a soaring sky adapts to my own horizon.

Mediterranean

from the Spanish of Jorge Guillén

A young one, vulnerably half naked, stretched
towards the intense, light-splintering waves of noon
on the hot sand of this Mediterranean beach,
turns and submits to the despotic sun —

exhibiting her rich, harmonious beauty
like a votive offering of health and youth
in honour of a sun god; while I try
to think how *I'd* respond to so much faith.

Completely at her ease, content for ever,
her limbs betray a knowledge of the fervour
and fierce concentration the sun's rays

consecrate to her body from above.
Unmoving, she receives their violent love
like the nymph of ancient myth she really is.

Dust

from the Spanish of Jorge Guillén

Road-dusty olives where the earth
raises its holes and bumps; beneath
the bright car a dense retinue —
blown planet in air sun-lit, a new
grey on the ancient olive grey.

A Hot October

from the Spanish of Jorge Guillén

> *Bring me, although it's autumn, nightingales.*
> — Góngora

Though stripping themselves bit by bit
the woods are golden now, the yellow leaf
glowing more warmly than the green did.
You've still got time to fall in love.

The Aspern Papers

from the Spanish of Jorge Guillén

Retired even from memories she lives on
reigning alone over her past
and famous what with the love
so much her own,
so intimate, night after night,
and the words of her poet
published at last, admired at last.

She was the inspiration once
of a man who strove
to create ideal beauty.
Now there she is in her house,
not a ghost, not a creature
of the imagination
but a real woman in a real body.

She's still her private self beside
the living water, once the Muse
of a poetry that, flown
from its secret nest, rose
to the heights far above
its forgotten grove.
                            Not
everything has to be spoken;
not everything has to be known.

White Cloud

from the German of Bertolt Brecht, 1898-1956

One evening in the blue month of September
we lay at peace beneath an apple bough.
I took her in my arms, my gentle lover,
and held her closely like a dream come true —
while far up in the tranquil summer heaven
there was a cloud, I saw it high and clear;
it was so white and so immense above us
and, as I watched, it was no longer there.

Since then so very many different evenings
have drifted blindly past in the general flow;
perhaps the apple orchards have been flattened,
and if you ask me where the girl is now
I have to admit I really don't remember.
I can imagine what you're going to say
but even her face I truly can't recapture,
I only know I kissed it there that day.

Even the kiss I would have long forgotten
if that one cloud had not been up there too —
I see it and will always see it plainly,
so white and unexpected in the blue.
Perhaps the apple boughs are back in blossom,
maybe she holds a fourth child on her knees;
the cloud, though, hung there for a moment only
and, as I watched, it broke up in the breeze.

Svendborg

from the German of Bertolt Brecht

We've lashed oars on the thatch
to keep it down in everything
short of a cyclone, and
the sun gilds our garden;
but deadly visions hang
like rain clouds in the sound.

A little boat with patched
sails skates on the crinkly
tinfoil of the bay; but we
are not deceived by scenery.
Ears cocked, we can hear
screams beyond the frontier.

The owl announces death
from the foliage these spring
nights while I read *Macbeth*,
Kant, or the *Tao Te Ching*;
twice daily the starlings
are silenced by a shriek

of ordnance from the naval
war games of the Reich.
The whitewash is peeling
from the damp ceiling
as I work at *Galileo*
in the converted stable.

Tacked to the oak beams,
a stage poster from
the old Schiffbauerdamm,
faded now, proclaims

the truth is concrete.
Confucius' scroll portrait,

the ashtrays, cigar boxes
and drawers of microfilm
make everything familiar:
from here I can watch
her strong form gardening,
the children at the swing.

This could be home from home
if things were otherwise:
twice daily the mails come
up the sound in a ship.
I notice that the house
has four doors for escape.

On a Drowned Girl

from the German of Bertolt Brecht

After she perished and went drifting down
from streams to wider waters, towards the coast,
the wondrous opal of the heavens shone
as though to propitiate her sodden ghost.

Algae and weeds embraced her thighs and hands
so that she grew much heavier in limb.
Pike coolly nibbled at her pale flesh; plants
and river-life weighed down her final swim.

The evening sky grew dark as if with smoke
and night hung out its bright stars once again;
as became evident when daylight broke
dawn and dusk, night and day, would still go on.

While her bruised body decomposed down there
it happened that, very slowly, God too forgot her —
first her face, then her hands, and last her hair;
then she was bones with other bones in the water.

On Swimming in Lakes and Rivers

from the German of Bertolt Brecht

In bleaching summer when winds up below
breathe only in the leaves of the treetops
we want to swim in lakes and rivers like
the waterweed, dark haunts of hidden pike.
Bodies grow light in water. When an elbow
slips naturally from water into sky
a faint breeze dandles it distractedly,
mistaking it for a broken bough perhaps.

The sky at noon bestows an immense calm.
You blink when a swift suddenly goes by.
Cold bubbles rising where the mud is warm
show that a fish rose a split second ago.
Trunk and thighs, the muscles resting, lie
afloat on the surface, silently at one.
Casual perch and trout go flicking through;
you feel, burning beyond the trees, the sun.

At dusk, having grown lazy and apathetic
drifting so long, your limbs begin to fret.
You have to smash it up, with a good kick,
into blue ripples that dash hither and yon;
but it's best to hang in there until sunset
for then the pale sharkskin clouds will come,
greedy and sinister on pond and pine,
and everything take on its proper form.

All you've to do is lie flat on your back,
as if from force of habit, and play dead.
You needn't swim, no, just behave as though
you belong with the gravel on the river bed.

You have to look up at the sky and act
exactly as if a woman held you tight —
without commotion, like the dear Lord God
who swims his rivers in the evening light.

Barbara

from the French of Jacques Prévert, 1900-1977

Barbara remember
it poured continuously on Brest that day
and you came smiling through the rain
radiant rapturous dripping wet
Barbara remember
I saw you in the rue de Siam
you smiled and I smiled too
even if you don't know who I am
Barbara remember
you whom I never knew
nor you me even so
remember don't forget
the young man in a doorway
sheltering from the downpour
who called your name Barbara
you ran to him in the rain
rapturous radiant dripping wet
and flung yourself in his arms
Barbara remember that
and don't mind if I talk to you
like this I always talk like this
to those I love even if I've only
seen them once I always talk
like this to those in love
even if we've never met
Barbara never forget
the happy quiet rain
on your happy face
on the happy town
the rainfall on the sea
on the dockyard on the island boat
Oh Barbara damn the war
I wonder where you are

after the rain of iron
of steel and blood and fire
and he who took you in his arms
so lovingly has he gone
is he dead is he still alive
Oh Barbara it has poured all day
on ruined Brest as it did before
but it's not the same any more
in these dire desolate rains
and now the storm is past
of steel and blood and iron
there are only clouds that burst
like dead dogs in the drains
that drift away disperse
in a downpour from the west
and break up far from Brest
nothing of which remains.

Antarctica

from the Spanish of Pablo Neruda, 1904-1973

Austral crown, concourse of frozen lights!
Cinder forest of ice dislodged
from the earth skin, re-opening nave
of a blue-green cathedral, crusher
of glass crystals, sub-zero
cliff of nocturnal snow,

grant me your double surface
stirred by victorious vacancy,
your furious wind race, lost horns
of shipwrecks and sunken worlds,
your storm-polished shield
a clear plate of quartz;

your unbreathable frost, your infinite
glittering minerals, empty
air without soil or poverty.
Realm of the harshest meridian,
whispering, dozing icicle harp
against the hostile stars,

the round oceans have concentrated
all their transparency in you,
you are strewn with their salt
castles and cities, a blizzard
roams your gritty solitude
like a snow-scorched jaguar.

Peril grows from your cupolas,
your flowing glacier; life
on your desolate spine is no richer

than a vineyard under the sea,
smoking but unconsumed
and saving its fire for spring.

Winter Garden

from the Spanish of Pablo Neruda

Winter, and slow leaves clothed
in silence and yellow
give resplendent dictation.

I'm a book of snow,
an open hand, a wide meadow,
a hopeful horizon;
I belong to the earth and its winter.

The murmur of the world rose in the branches.
The months went by, the fugitive
sky was a bowl of summer
and the driving cloud dispersed.

As if the past were back, with its childhood ivy,
I waited in grief on the balcony
for the earth to stretch its wings
over my disinhabited love.

I knew the rose would wilt,
the seasonal peach-stone sleep and increase;
I drank air until
the whole sea went dark
and the rainbow turned to ashes.

But the world lives on,
softening its interrogation,
stretching the skin of its silence.
Come from afar, I'm taciturn now,
enveloped in cold rain and bells.
To the pure death of the earth I owe
my wish to germinate and grow.

from Burbles

from the French of Samuel Beckett, 1906-1989

do not forget when in Tangier
St. Andrew's Church and Cemetery
the dead doubly buried beneath
scatterings of flower and leaf
a bench raised to the memory
of Arthur Keyser as for you
still up and under take a pew
and sit with him in spirit here

one farther on commemorates
Caroline Hay Taylor who
for ever true to her belief
that there is hope while there is life
quit Ireland for the pearly gates
in August nineteen thirty-two

The Same Ardour

from the French of Jean-F. Brière, 1909-1992

on a Georgia lynching

One of the crowd, black brother, I look up
from Haiti, one more in the long cortège —
as poor as you, as sad, as great, a black drop
circulating in the same new upsurge.

Black heroes both, yourself as black as I,
our struggles down the years of genocide
shared the same wretched fate; hung out to dry,
our shadows mingled at the same roadside.

A child of the slave ships, unreconciled,
like me you feel the agony afresh
reviving at the rope's end, and the old
scars re-opening in your wounded flesh.

The same fierce revolutionary vertigo,
the same mirages, wavered in your eye;
although we parted centuries ago
I know your outline on the crimson sky.

As once in the long miserable age
under the whiplash, the historic yoke,
your life-affirming cry tears at its cage
and I myself stop breathing as you choke.

We have unlearnt the dialect of the tribe.
You rap in jive talk at the ancient wrong,
my chagrin twitching to your bluesy vibe.
I speak your sorrow in a foreign tongue —

but the blows you get keep stinging my own skin,
a hanged man's shadow darkens my own mind;
the same rage rises in your heart and mine
from the hot woodpile, fiery and condoned.

When you cough blood it spatters my own shirt
and I myself give vent to your wild scream.
With the same ardour, in the same dark night,
black brother, we're both dreaming the same dream.

Trout in the Water

from the Italian of Mario Luzi, 1914-2005

It whets her senses, combs her thought,
this water-flow, this air-flow; vast,
it braces her for a leap and springs
some wavery memory, short-term,
long-term, of icy glimmerings.
Crazy, disorienting, the spate
cradles and thrashes her in turn,
ruffling the present and the past,
confusing time and space. She dives
to her obscure initiatives,
balancing there in muddy clouds,
chasing volition fast or slow
among the silent weeds below,
the emerald dark reviving her;
and look, she flings herself on high
through the grey glass, into the air,
dividing weight from shadow, thuds
and snaps the fine resurgent line
to brightness and transparency.

    The river — weaving, varying — splits
her vision up and multiplies,
with a perpetual change of lights
and their refractions, what she sees
around its fluent, glittering skin.
The waters dazzle here and there
but clasp her tightly, take her in,
open each turbulent barrier,
whirling and eddying, and wrap
her rippling body in a cape
of power and frenzy, urging her
on to her destiny —
           except

she has no destiny, not she,
but a generic energy.

The Arno, does it know or does
the ever-present thought that thinks
there in its place? She rises, sinks,
sustained and checked, received again
into that breezy, quivering reach,
her own true element, true to which
from room to room she comes and goes
along the lengthening stream of time.

Do they exist or do we dream,
in our own human pain, those spun
heavens, always compliant, free?
Does the desire for them explain
those exultations?
River-daughter,
be she compliant or not, she rides
the strength of the dim current, hides
and dozes in the shallow water;
rests in a pool between two rocks
and dances sometimes in the rain
or thrills to a fresh flowery dawn
of bulging faces, splashing foam.
She knows and not-knows, like the depths
themselves, her closely clinging home,
since it's their wisdom to belong
to greater wisdom, even perhaps
not-knowing the question that still breaks
the silence and picks up its song.

from Gramsci's Ashes

from the Italian of Pier Paolo Pasolini, 1922-1975

There's nothing spring-like in this toxic air
which further darkens or with a bright glitter
blinds the dark garden of the foreigner
and nothing spring-like in the soapy cloud
casting its veil on the vast amphitheatre
of yellow attics ranged beside the mud
of the Tiber and among the purple pines.
Autumnal springtime spreads a mortal peace,
though disabused like all our destinies,
over exhausted ruins where the strong
ingenuous impulse to start life anew
crumbled; and now silence, hot but hard,
where a motorbike whines off into the blue.
A boy in that far spring when even wrong
was at least vigorous, that Italian spring
our parents knew, vital with earth and song
and so much less distracted, when the place
united in fanaticism, you outlined
already, brother, with your skinny hand
the ideal society whose light shines forth
in this dark garden although not for us
since we lie dead with you in the wet earth.
There remains now for you only a long
rest here in the 'non-Catholic' cemetery,
a last internment though this time among
boredom and privilege; and the only cries
you hear are a few final anvil-blows
from an industrial neighbourhood which rise
in the evening over wretched roofs, a grey
rubble of tin cans and scrap metal where
with a fierce song a boy rounds out his day
grinning, while the last rain falls everywhere.

Streams and Woods

from the French of Philippe Jaccottet, 1925-2021

I

The brightness of these March woods is unreal,
everything still so fresh it hardly insists.
Not many birds yet; but where whitethorn
quickens the thickets a cuckoo sings,
and sparkling smoke carries away
whatever it was that was burnt today.
Dead leaves will make the living crown.
At the end of the shadiest paths,
among brambles, you will find an anemone
bright and ordinary like the morning star.

2

Even if I could examine the cobweb intricacies
of my nervous system, I would still
be able to praise these wooden
columns, even those chosen for destruction.

If the beauty of March consists in the obedience
of blackbird and violet to a clear sky,
I too must extend my confidence one day
to the lightning-flash of the axe.

3

Sunday fills the woods with complaining children,
ageing women, boys with bloody knees
and dirty handkerchiefs; and the pond
is littered with crumpled newspapers.

Shouts fade with the light; under the elms
a girl tugs resentfully at her skirt
if anyone passes. All gentleness, of the air
or of love, is harsh on the other side:
fine Sundays have their price, like parties
that leave wine-stains on the table at daybreak.

All this anxiety is beside the point,
my walking in these woods will not be long,
and words are neither more nor less useful
than the willows rustling in the marshes.

Dust-destined, yes, but the dust glitters;
other mortals will walk here when I'm gone.
As for the death of beauty, that hardly matters,
it shines forth in its very abdication.

Daybreak

from the French of Philippe Jaccottet

1

Night is not what we think, the reverse of fire,
sun-death and the negation of the light,
but a subterfuge intended to discover
whatever remains invisible in daylight.

The zealous servants of the visible
having withdrawn, the violet has made
its home now in the deepening shade,
the final refuge of the exiled soul.

2

Like the oil asleep in the lamp which suddenly,
beneath a moon swept by a flight of birds,
transforms itself to a glow and breathes,
you murmur and burn; and no voice
can convey the pure quality of it.
You are the light rising on cold rivers,
the lark sprung from the field;
the very earth is laid bare and elated.

3

I speak to you, daybreak, although all I say
is only a flight of words in the air.
Light is fugitive, embrace it
and it becomes a shade; yet once
again, as if it had heard my prayer,
the sun rises and sends forth its first light.

Patience

from the French of Philippe Jaccottet

In the playing-cards spread out in the lamplight
like the powdery wings of fallen moths
I see beyond the smoke-wreathed tablecloths
something that would be better kept from sight —
a new insomnia the rung glasses chime,
fear of being afraid, contraction of time,
bodily attrition, collapse of resistance.
Old men discard their previous existence,
quelling a qualm, and turn to contemplate
the hailstones slashing at the garden gate.

The Voice

from the French of Philippe Jaccottet

What is it that sings when the other voices are silent?
Whose is that pure low voice, that sibilant song?
Is it down the road on a snow-covered lawn
or close at hand, unaware of an audience?
This is the mysterious first bird of dawn.
Do you hear the voice increase in volume
and, as a March wind quickens a creaking tree,
sing mildly to us without fear,
content in the fact of death? Do you hear?
What does it sing in the grey dawn? Nobody knows
but the voice is audible only to those
whose hearts seek neither possession nor victory.

Ignorance

from the French of Philippe Jaccottet

The older I grow the more ignorant I become,
the longer I live the less I possess or control.
All I have is a little space, snow-dark
or glittering, never inhabited.
Where is the giver, the guide, the guardian?
I sit in my room and am silent; silence
arrives like a servant to clean things up
while I wait for the lies to disperse.
And what remains to this dying man
that so well prevents him from dying?
What does he find to say to the four walls?
I hear him talking still, and his words
come in with the dawn, imperfectly understood:

'Love, like fire, can only reveal its brightness
on the failure and the beauty of burnt wood.'

The Gipsies

from the French of Philippe Jaccottet

There are fires under the trees —
you can hear the low voice of the tribe
on the fringes of cities.

If, short-lived souls that we are,
we pass silently
on the dark road tonight,
it is for fear you should die,
perpetual murmur
around the hidden light.

Words in the Air

from the French of Philippe Jaccottet

The clear air said: 'I was your home once
but other guests have taken your place:
where will you go who liked it here so much?
You looked at me through the thick dust
of the earth, and your eyes were known to me.
You sang sometimes, you even whispered low
to someone else who was often asleep,
you told her the light of the earth
was too pure not to point a direction
which somehow avoided death. You imagined
yourself advancing in that direction
but now I no longer hear you. What have you done?
Above all, what is your lover going to think?'

And she, his friend, replied through tears of happiness:
'He has changed into the shade that pleased him best.'

'(Nothing at all, a footfall on the road . . . '

from the French of Philippe Jaccottet

(Nothing at all, a footfall on the road,
but more mysterious than guide or god.)

Glimpses

from the French of Philippe Jaccottet

The children run shouting
in the thick grass of the playground.

The tall tranquil trees
and the torrential light
of a September morning
protect them still from the anvil
sparkling with stars up there.

⤳

The soul, so chilly, so fierce, must it really
trudge up this glacier for ever,
solitary, in bare feet, no longer
remembering even its childhood prayer,
its coldness for ever punished by this cold?

⤳

Wrapped in a blue bath-robe
which is wearing out too,
she goes to a mirror round
like the mouth of a child
who doesn't know how to lie.

Hair the colour of ash now
in the slow burn of time;

and yet the morning sun
quickens her shadow still.

⤳

At the window with its freshly whitewashed frame
(to keep out flies, to keep out ghosts)
the white head of an old man leans
over a letter or the local news.
Against the wall dark ivy grows.

Save him, ivy and lime, from the dawn wind,
from long nights and the other, eternal night.

The Word Joy

from the French of Philippe Jaccottet

I am searching here in the fog
for something escaped from the fog
having heard steps in the distance
and the voices of passers-by.

～

Perhaps I imagined it, the sunset brush
on the rough canvas of earth,
a golden evening oil
on fields and woods; but it looked
like lamplit bread on a kitchen table.

～

Each day, perhaps, you might replace
the stitches in the severed net —
thus, in the distances of space,
to sew up, star by star, the night.

～

These bonfires in the February gardens
lit less for order, you would say,
than to help spread the light,
can we ourselves manage no more
than this with our secret heart?

～

Show me the man who has found certitude
and shines in peace like the last

peak to fade at twilight, never
wincing under the weight of night.

To Henry Purcell

from the French of Philippe Jaccottet

Listen: how is it
that our troubled voice mingles like this
with the stars?

He has scaled the heavens
on rungs of glass
by the youthful grace of his art.

～

We hear the passing of ewes
who throng the dust of the celestial summer,
whose milk we have never drunk.

He has herded them into the fold of night
where straw shines among the stones,
and the gate bangs shut.
The coolness of these quiet grasses for ever . . .

～

What do we hear
who tune in to the night?
A leisurely snow
of crystal.

～

Imagine a comet
returning centuries hence
from the kingdom of the dead,
crossing our century tonight
and sowing the same seeds . . .

While I listen
the reflection of a candle
flickers in the mirror
like a flame woven
of water.

Might not this voice be the echo
of another, more real?
And will that ever be heard
by those thrashing in terror?
Will I hear it myself?

If ever they speak above us
in the starry trees of their April.

❧

You are seated before
the tense loom of the harp.

I know you, though invisible,
weaver of supernatural streams.

Silhouette

from the French of Annette M'Baye (born 1926)

Sun behind and shadow before!
A calabash on a proud head,
a breast, a fluttering strip of cloth,
two feet brushing new shapes in the sand.

Dakar

Loango Strand

from the French of Jean-Baptiste Tati-Loutard, 1938-2009

I've followed them as far as this Congo strand
by a scent of blood, the hot scent of my own,
ignoring the other raw wounds left behind
in the bad times by a whipping wind. I stand
here, sick of the whole thing. I can't go on.
The very footpath hesitates at this point
in distant memory of their last descent;
the ocean, visible from the final wharf,
still appears infinite and it still skies
its breakers as it's done for centuries
beyond the impartial thunder of the surf.
God's spirit moves still on the waters' face,
a vast dumb platitude and hovering place
for cruising gulls. I won't be going ahead
with my grim pilgrimage in the dismal ditch
of a dark seabed paved with skull and bone
west to Virginia's fresh resurgent beach
and cotton-flowery factory fields of graves.
We shall erect our own high cenotaphs
to the belated rest of the chained dead
herded aboard, who even this evening retch
black bile in the grey chaos of the waves.

Autumn in Grignan

from the French of Denis Rigal, 1938-2021

for Philippe Jaccottet

The gentle southern air still breathes each day
through yellow beeches as the light withdraws
from a blazing rustle of wild-cherry trees.
A great grey heron makes its careful way
darting now here, now there, its precise beak
for tiny creatures in the gathering mist.
The man, pausing beside the road, turns back
from a traditional ox-cart creaking past,
the axles of the same old local freight.
He puts a hand out to an orchard gate
(*Bonjour, monsieur Gauguin!*), points to a dark
second growth beneath apple branches twisted
by some mysterious pain and to the kindly
little valleys where there still persist
a little thyme yet for a little time,
some bare-field lavender in wilting rows
and grapes to gather after the first frost
that make this pale white wine, this quiet wine.

Blinding Light

from the French of Denis Rigal

Mankind is a wistful, trudging beast
upon whose many doubts the vast
no-colour is bestowed, devolves —
that layer of hard, blinding light
which falls on rocks and rustling waves,
on busy ports and quiet coves,
astonishes and vanishes.

It leaves a floating veil behind it,
meaningful, with turquoise glances,
on a world hidden from our gaze:
nude beauty, hesitant distances
the weightless blue of these last days.

Even So

from the French of Denis Rigal

Who dares to speak in the ruins,
who will sing now among
the black stones of disaster?
A solitary coryphaeus
perched alone on a crumbling plinth?

What taut string will replace
our plaintive voice
at the high note where it breaks off?
Look at these millions of shadows
each with its soul
in a bundle of rags
(all the childhood memories)
skirting the heavy, unfordable streams.

And who, knowing this, knowing
the end, will even so
live on with the imponderables
in the tremors of earthly desire?

Lines for Li Po

from the French of Denis Rigal

The emperor and the sage, enchanted both,
and the lovely lady in brocade cloth
are numbed by the same bitter breeze.
Ignore the yellow dog and the dust
of the world, the crescent moon is a frost-
bright blade to sever heads, snuff out
faces; and the boat drifts expectedly
towards a framed-in-the-sunset tree
where all power and its fine phrases
finish, with no 'limits of love and light'.

Sensation

from the French of Ivonne Bolumbu (born 1951)

An insanely happy sensation has seized me,
the predisposition to an uncontagious
epidemic of joy, and this indolent ease,
an ease such as I haven't known for ages,
arriving uninvited some time last night
to burst out in my being and give me pause
like the first symptom of I don't know what
incurable malady, this wild delight
born of I don't know what venial sin
torments me and upsets my chronic woes.
I should engrave my gratitude in your skull
or paint this brief elation on your back
for it's too acute and it will vanish soon.
My dubious paradise is quite unreasonable,
all this good fortune is a pain in the neck.

Paranoia

from the Irish of Nuala Ní Dhomhnaill (born 1952)

The old woman of the mill
scrubs bloody clothes in the river,
glancing in my direction
a little too often.
A dog barks and barks
at the end of the house;
the church bells are muffled;
a hooded crow flies in my face.
It's high time I got out of here.

Down in the village
the people eye me furtively;
they lower their heads
and avoid me like the plague.
A whirlwind raises the hair
on the necks of the hills,
rain thuds in the earth
and a snowstorm begins.
I slam the door of my house
on the lot of them.

. . . And start awake in the night
surrounded by sulphurous light
while the ceiling grows slowly bright
in the dripping dawn.
The bedroom door swings open of its own accord
and a hound bounds into the room at me
this very minute,
his two eyes the size of plates —
no, bigger, of cartwheels;
no, bigger, of whirling windmills.

An Orphan at the Door

from the Irish of Nuala Ní Dhomhnaill

As fragile as a shell
cast up on a rocky shore,
I stand outside your door
in the afternoon. The bell
rings deep in your house,
echoing in the long, empty rooms.

The kitchen radio howls
rock music and, for a moment,
I feel a surge of hope before
I realize it's only on
to deter thieves, and a long
wait lies before me
with no sound of your step.

I ring again and the echo climbs
among high ceilings, wooden stairs.
Peering through the letter box
I recognize in the Georgian proportions
an intricate crystal structure
that bodies forth and hides a god.

A red rose stands in a vase
on the hall table, a sweater
hangs from the banister;
unopened letters lie about
carelessly on the floor
but nowhere is there a sign
of you to be seen.

Over the drawing-room fireplace
a postcard from your lover
boasts that hers is the first

mail in your new house. It shows
a simple tourist view
of the tumulus at Newgrange.

There is a reference (not lost
on you, of course)
to the *hieros gamos*, the marriage
made in heaven; outside
the warm conspiracy of your love
I stand, a nobody,
an orphan at the door.

An icy wind blows through the cold porches
of the farthest pavilions
in the depths of my soul,
the rivers of emotion are frozen solid;
my heart beats wildly
like strange and treacherous seas.

Damn my wooden head, my feather brain,
why am I waiting here
at your closed door?
When the bell peals inside
like the Angelus, do I really
expect the sky to open and a dove
to descend upon me from above?

It's only in the soul
that the miracles take place
of love, forgiveness and grace;
it's only in dream truth
that the sun and moon shine
together in a bright sky
while day dawns on them both.

The Race

from the Irish of Nuala Ní Dhomhnaill

Like a mad lion, like a demented bull, like one
of the wild boar in the Fenian cycle
or the hero leaping upon the giant
with his fringe of whistling silk,
I drive at high speed through
the small midland towns of Ireland,
catching up with the wind ahead
while the wind behind me whirls and dies.

Like a shaft from a bow, like a shot from a gun
or a sparrowhawk in a sparrow throng
on a March day, I scatter the road signs,
miles or kilometres what do I care.
Nenagh, Roscrea, Portlaoise,
I pass through them in a daze:
they are only speed limits put there
to hold me up on my way to you.

Through mountain cleft, bogland and wet pasture
I race impetuously from west to east —
a headlong flight in your direction,
a quick dash to be with you.
The road rises and falls before me,
surface changing from grit to tar;
I forget geography, all I know
is the screech of brakes and the flash of lights.

Suddenly, in the mirror, I catch sight of the sun
glowing red behind me on the horizon,
a vast blazing crimson sphere like the heart
of the Great Cow of the Smith God

when she was milked through a sieve,
the blood dripping as in a holy picture.
Thrice red, it is so fierce it pierces
my own heart, and I catch my breath in pain.

I keep glancing anxiously at the dripping sun
while trying to watch the road ahead
as Briar Rose must have glanced
at her finger after the spindle
of the spinning-wheel had pricked her,
turning it round and round as if in a trance.
When Deirdre saw the calf's blood on the snow
did it ever dawn on her what the raven was?

Oh, I know it's to you that I'm driving,
my lovely man, the friend of my heart,
and the only things between us tonight
are the road sign and the traffic light;
but your impatience is like a stone
dropping upon us out of the sky;
and add to that our bad humour,
gaucherie, and the weight of my terrible pride.

Another great weight is descending upon us
if things turn out as expected, a weight
greater by far than the globe of the sun
that bled in my mirror a while back —
and thou, dark mother, cave of wonders,
since it's to you that we spin on our violent course,
is it true what they say that your kiss is sweeter
than Spanish wine, Greek honey, or the golden mead
    of the Norse?

The Clifden Road

from the French of Michel Houellebecq (born 1956)

West of Clifden on a cliff
where sky changes into sea
and sea to memory as if
at the edge of a new world

on the long hills of Clifden
the green hills of Clifden
I will lay down my grief.

To accept death it must be
that death changes into light
that light changes into sea
and sea into memory.

The far west of human life
lies on the Clifden road
the long Clifden road
where man lays down his grief
between the waves and the light.

The Dark Garden

from the French of Michel Houellebecq

We walked into a ferny garden where
everything seemed much quieter than before.
Once through the wicket, we saw no more sun;
each wandered the deserted path alone.

You glanced uneasily, you caught your breath
as a slick snake slid to the undergrowth;
amidst all that chaotic vegetation
the flowers put on a petal exhibition.

Impatient creatures, we roam paradise
haunted by sorrow, conscious of disgrace,
the thought of sex persistently to the fore.
We are, we exist, we want to exist some more,

nothing to lose; but plant life, so resigned,
brings sinister, invasive death to mind.
In a dark garden the body decomposes;
our decomposing bodies drown in roses.

Existence

from the French of Michel Houellebecq

Clearly this stupid world doesn't inspire
anything now but an intense antipathy,
an urge to vanish and be done with it;
you hardly dare pick up a newspaper.

Perhaps we should go back to the old home
where our ancestors lived under the eye
of heaven, and find the curious harmony
that sanctified their lives from womb to tomb.

It's some kind of faith for which we yearn,
some gentle web of close dependencies
transcending and containing our existence.
We can no longer live so far from the eternal.

The Peace of Objects

from the French of Michel Houellebecq

The peace of objects, strange phenomenon,
not even on speaking terms.
Time wears us down
while they remain
at rest; nothing bothers them.

They alone watch over our doubtful hours,
our lonely nights and days,
taking the grim colours
of our old dolours,
our unadventurous ways.

Inert, on us too our existence weighs,
no pardon, no reprieve.
Nothing on earth relieves
this glum dismay,
this sense of banishment.

Defined by objects made in our own image,
through them we live our lives.
Meanwhile, deep down, there hides
a buried memory
of having once been gods.

A Year of Grace

from the French of Monique Mbeka (born 1962)

I'm getting a year of grace
for my year of pain and rage,
my year of famine —
a year to study film
production in Kinshasa
and finally come of age.

My year of grace is beautiful
for framing my young ideas,
my hopes and fears;
for giving me leave to love
the world around me and a soul
pierced by a thousand stars.

The world declares itself in words,
my pen has come alive.
My old diaries babble
that life is horrible,
I'll never write so well again,
only the same poems over and over;

but I've better things to do
than who what where when.
We are as 'free' as ever
we hoped, and I'm writing this while you complain.

APPENDIX

RAW MATERIAL

from the Hindi of 'Gopal Singh' (1959-2020)

A Child of the Forest

A child of the forest, I roam city slums.
Dinner clatters, the *cuit*, the *cru*;
dhal simmers on cow-dung fires,
samosas fry beneath tangled wires
in a thousand frugal homes.

A shack in the woods and a few
bamboo sticks would do
but I keep coming
back to life
whose blaze darkens the stars.

Tata. Maruti. IndiCom. IndiGo.
Bavinder Ready Cash. Dubai
is Closer than You Know.
Unwind Beneath the Goa Sky.

The raw stuff of the future
sighs as I drive home
at the cow-dust hour
past twinkling compounds,
building sites
and forests of billboards.

New Retina Solutions.
Think Skin. Gitanjali.
Embrace the Spiritual
to Beat the Credit Crunch.

Asphalt Roads

The sun bangs like a gun on Rajasthan,
the sandstone fort, the asphalt road,
the desert. Rain drums in the mud
and flashes like a sword
above the plain;
mists rise like ghosts or scents
from lanes, tanks, palm thatch,
palm and pine.
Time lives in a stagnant pond
that sees cloud best
and a periwinkle sky beyond.

Those who scrape and scratch
a life from the soil watch
the clicking corn seethe,
the rice, the maize
awaiting the quick scythe.

When the monsoon relents
and the opaque past
vanishes, wind rises
and sings to a blind old man
crouched in the luminous dust
where he began,
imagining a future.

Raw Material

The recycling of old shoes
as raw material
makes artwork
of the contingent real
when sunlight,
finding them
among shadows,
throws
shadow shapes on their used souls.

Only material forms die
says the *Gita*,
the dusty soul within
alone survives
even as we discard
one body for another.
Avatar and aviator,
I who was once a virus,
once a mosquito,
begin to re-imagine
my previous lives.

My previous lives were long ago
in Chittagong and Kathmandu
but there is life to come
when we rejoin the dust

or drift downstream
and sink into the sand like foam.

Plant Life

The plants grow audibly at night
whispering among themselves
about their private lives,
the wild love in the leaves,
the nectar in the flower,
remembering the clear
spring meadows of Kashmir
and the lost horizons of Tibet.

As they evolve in knowing growth
and time-lapse circumspection
they slowly learn to shun
the shade and find the sun;
but this is not enough.

The flowers want to be tough,
to think and propagate,
escape from the close earth,
the traditional dark fate,
chase space and light
and share the world above.

Slow Clouds

Elsewhere they race for show.
Here in the hills they're high and slow
condensing rain to give
fulfilment to the leaves
on the earth below
and to their own vague lives.
The lilac listens to the thunder too.

I turned to clouds to avoid
a world of hectoring voices,
search-and-destroy devices.
Now iCloud, 'cloud services'
weigh on us like the void.

So few alternatives
but here in the hills they go
for a short while at their own pace
imagining earthly peace.

Wind and Strings

Pearly sitar, your dewy strings
glittering in the wind, sun-struck,
asleep but stirring, stretched tight
on a cane chair left out last night,
your hum echoes the stars, it rings
dim chords, a plangent music like
trains that we no longer take.

Dharma Bums

Those who raise their eyes
to the beautiful words
— 'contentment', 'paradise' —
can never . . . *Dharma?*
What do they know
of dharma, these spoilt kids
without warmth, without charm?
Eternity takes time.

They sit like tramps
beside the road,
each on a dusty bum,
when they should be at home
in advertising.

Advertising the benefits
of our spirituality —
Ganesh the god of profit,
Saraswati the celebrant of it,
Rama of many dominions
and Krishna, 'brighter than a thousand suns'.

A New Earth

We hid, heads in a cloud,
till the worst was over.
A perpendicular
rain curtain covered
the nightbound countryside.

As day broke a redstart
chip-chattered to the light
of a new earth on Earth.
Parrot and squirrel
drink from the same bird table;

and wasted fields steam
in the rising sun,
their violent ruination
grounds for a new fruition
as they become
bright gardens of winged dreams.

Water

If everything is water as the Greek said
the woman at the dhobi ghat
flapping laundry by dawn light
knows more than most
of future, past,
the living and the dead.

Hers is the articulate flute
of thaw water that runs downstream
with twigs and leaves, dead cows
and recent contamination
— E. coli, cryptosporidium —
her dream
not the white snows
of Sikkim and Tibet
but point-of-use filtration.

Which doesn't mean a bleak reductionism
since the old gods live on —
not on the high peaks
perhaps, but everywhere day breaks
on water and a washerwoman
sings to her own reflection.

Mark Rothko

'unknown adventures in an unknown space'

Bacteria drink sunlit bacteria
amid mud clouds; winds dance
and shake the rustling rice
in depths of field and hue;
the god, the divine instance,
almost reveals his hidden face.

Rough-edged, gruff, block upon block,
the great sea has gone out
leaving salt marshes, rock,
vague ripples to the horizon,
silence, colour cloud upon cloud,
brush strokes of intuition.

Red tide, rain on a twilit ocean?
God on television?
It looks dim and simple
yet is as decorative
as a Tamil temple
or Goanese baroque.

Behind the portals though
the spiritual narrative,
behind the torn veil
a rich interior glow
as of an absent presence
still desperate to get through.

Recycling Song

Swords into ploughshares, us
to birds and bushes, everyone
to topsoil in the end.
Be careful with that refuse,
respect that wrapper; once
in another life that bottle was your friend.

'What goes around . . .' The *Gita*
warns us that we never die,
something escapes the blaze.
Our smoke and methane rise
above the world of matter
in viral columns to a busy sky.

Throw nothing out; recycle
the vilest rubbish, even
your own discarded page.
Everything comes full circle:
see you again in heaven
some sunny evening in a future age.

Coco-de-Mer

So many strange species in the spice isles,
none stranger than ourselves
with our urge, evident from the word go,
to compensate for a sweaty brow
by giving stick to the slow
mule and the donkey going round.

Tired of the same springs watering the same ground,
the peace, the over-abundant choice of fruit —
crab apple, mango, guava, pomegranate
with the dew still upon it —
and desperate to escape we found
the gates locked on the outside and a grim
rota of vigilant cherubim
to ensure we endure our fate.

'Where art thou?' A once familiar voice.
But still we chew on the womb-shaped coco-de-mer
(delicious source, goes one theory,
of our euphoria and despair),
wondering why it was planted here
in the first place
if not to tempt us into time and history.

On the Blink

With civilized discourse on the blink
and hope abandoned years ago
there's no point now in wasting ink
and energy complaining, though
the world would drive you to the drink.

The world would drive you to the brink
of frank despair, but let it go;
let the whole kit 'n' caboodle sink
to its destruction. As we know
it's later than we care to think.

The Great Wave

When it happened we were asleep in Bangalore
but later took a train and hired a car:
heroism or curiosity? I can't be positive
but a news instinct told us to be here.
A plate had shifted far beneath the sea
in distant Java, sending a great wave
to wreck the houses on this quiet shore.
A diffident wave breaks on the same shore

quietly this raw morning as if to say
it wouldn't hurt a fly much less destroy
a civilization, though it did just that —
hotels, schools and hospitals knocked flat
by a cliff of water smashing into the coast.
The swirling mud receded leaving a waste
of bodies, furniture, palm trunks, dereliction
and in the streets the contents of an ocean.

If 'waste is the new raw material' as they say
our resources are infinite: on black beaches
carrion, groceries, sewage, wide-open fridges
fought over by frenetic gull and crow.
Tractors haul the wreckage, dead car and cow,
balconies, splintered bits of bungalow.
On the last rock some soapstone Madurai
devotional figures . . . A post-tsunami sky.

Up at the Palace

for Anoushka Narain

Sixty-eight people died when a bomb went off
in the market place, but that was months ago.
The rest of us go on 'having our being'
in the packed streets of Jaipur, in the rough
neighbourhoods, the parks and tourist parts
of the pink city; while up at the city palace
a concert has been laid on for visitors —
ragas and Rameau under climbing stars.

The poets tell us about rooms where huge
cockroaches skitter over vile linoleum,
rats in the kitchen, scorpions in the cracks,
the Ganges choked with every kind of filth
and foghorns mourning from the Kidderpore Docks;
but we sip champagne, we nibble partridges
and follow the maharani to her pavilion
where a chamber orchestra is plucking strings.

The boy putting up posters for a pittance
and the Dalit girl-child tapping at Toyota
windows for spare change are not invited
to glitter among the balconies and arches
admiring Rajput pictures, marble elephants
and the ivory knick-knacks of the interior
but, like the crows, stare at our sumptuous
goings-on from the Govindji Temple.

The curse of karma keeps them in their places
gazing at lighted windows with rapt faces.
People, the terrible things you must have done
when you were soldiers of fortune, local kings

or naughty nautch girls in the old days!
Did you crush pearls for aphrodisiacs,
poison your cousins for a shaky throne
or cripple your tenants with a punitive tax?

No, you did nothing of the kind of course
but you were born into a dream of shame
whose violent colours filled the universe
and left you silent, each with a secret name,
listening to the music of other spheres.
You too will sip champagne one of these years
despite the old, self-perpetuating pantheon;
but what do we worship now the gods have gone?

Afterword

These aren't translations, in the strict sense, but *versions* of their originals devised, as often as not, from cribs of one kind or another. Some deplore this now common practice, insisting that the impersonation in English of poets in other tongues should be confined to those with a working knowledge of Greek or Russian, as the case may be — or indeed Spanish, Hebrew, Arabic, Igbo, Hindi or Chinese. (As for Hindi, my 'Raw Material' sequence owes so much to real Indian poems it must be considered unoriginal and so qualify for inclusion.) There's everything to be said for the real translator on whose work we rely. An important school of thought — Nabokov and Ted Hughes for example — used to insist on word for word translation. Nabokov: 'Any translation that does not sound like a translation is bound to be inexact upon inspection.' Hughes: 'As soon as devices extraneous to the original are employed for the purpose of recreating its "spirit", the value of the whole enterprise is called in question.' 'Better,' he says, 'the very oddity and struggling dumbness of a word for word version,' (*Modern Poetry in Translation*, 1965) — though his *Tales from Ovid* (1997) was guided by different principles. My own versions, looking to recreate the spirit and employing many extraneous devices, belong in another category, that of poems *adapted* from their originals, relying for instance on the scholarly work of A. C. Graham for the T'ang poems, and on that of Lucy Rosenstein for the Indian ones, to make something not only (I hope) fairly respectable but also readable, and perhaps re-readable, in a different language. I've taken many liberties, in the hope that the results will read *almost* like original poems in English, while allowing their sources to remain audible. 'To write is always to translate,' says José Saramago, 'even when we are using our own language . . . Our words convey mere fragments of the reality on which our experience fed.' With translation we're at *two* removes from the original impulse.

This was the case with, for example, my attempt at Valéry's 'Le Cimetière marin'. There were those, myself among them, who queried my title, 'The Seaside Cemetery', which sounds glib in English and seems to suggest somewhere right on the shore, or behind a beach, with kiddies and ice-cream; it's a tricky one. 'The Graveyard by the Sea' (Cecil Day Lewis)? Too sombre for such a paradoxically lively piece of work, except for those who dislike the word cemetery; and again, not quite right topographically. 'The Marine Cemetery', full of marines? No, as those who have ever set foot in Sète will know, Valéry's title is what the place is commonly called to distinguish it from the other, landward one. His is the *sea*-side cemetery. It's not on the shore exactly but up a hill above the shore, and it looks out over the sea. Its proper name is the Cimetière du Mont Saint-Clair. There are hundreds buried there including sailors, fishermen and their families; also Valéry himself, a son of the town, with an inscription from his poem:

> *O récompense après une pensée*
> *Qu'un long regard sur le calme des dieux!*

Begun in July, 1917, when so much change was taking place in Europe, and first published (*Nouvelle Revue française*) in 1920, the 'Cimetière' has long been a recognized classic — even, so to speak, a design classic. The vocabulary is fastidious, the shape of the poem perfect with a closed perfection. There's a shine on it; and the ten-syllable line, so lightweight to the alexandrine-minded French, adds the (in context) eccentric touch that makes all the difference. The challenge was somehow to indicate this virtuosity in English. No easy task, but an imagined kinship, however remote, perceived in a foreign text — Ovid's 'Corinnae concubitus' (*Amores* I, v), Pasternak's 'White Night' — will help, as will affinities of idea, shape and atmosphere. These are, in fact, what dictate your choice of poems in the first place, though a liking for seaside cemeteries can be enough to set you off.

Seen from one point of view, there's a peculiar impertinence involved in this kind of thing; but, to borrow a form of words from Elizabeth Bowen, who am I that I shouldn't have a go? A poem, says Yves Bonnefoy, isn't the end in itself but 'the meaning it bears'; let's not, he says, make a fetish of the printed page: 'Released from fixed form, which is merely its trace, the first intention or intuition can be tried out anew in another language . . . and on this second journey we have the right to be ourselves.' Poetry, in other words, isn't always lost in translation, even if 'the poetry' is; something, the thought, survives. Elsewhere he strikes a cautionary note: 'The translator will end up on a dark beach before a whole hyperborean world shrouded in fog; he knows he will never find the shore he dreamed of.' The historical moment can be relevant here. My 'Provençal' (really Occitan) sequence 'Women in Love', for example — acknowledgements to Meg Bogin, *The Women Troubadours* (Norton, 1980), a study of the *trobairitz* — is far removed in time and understanding from the lonely castles of the Languedoc hill country with their medieval amusements. The religious undertones and devotional subtexts usually attributed to *l'amour courtois* aren't in play here. The poems, mostly excerpted from longer, conversational pieces, have an air of negotiable transparency, but the voices can seem as remote as T'ang China or ancient Greece, those dreamt-of shores: faint echoes from antique groves.

Propertius, real translator Gilbert Highet, gets some rough treatment in my 'Sextus and Cynthia' exercise, as does Nerval in my 'Chimeras'. The more modern we get the less dubious I am about the results, and this is especially true of 19th- and 20th-century France. My own spoken French is a disgrace, but the likes of Corbière and Laforgue still speak to us clearly and companionably as contemporaries, perhaps because they were naturalized in English by Eliot and others — or rather, because there was already something anglophone in their tones of voice just waiting to be noticed. So, in a sort of back-formation, the Anglo-American idiom they 'helped' create accommodates them with ease. Coming forward in time, the same is true of Philippe Jaccottet, who can read like David Gascoyne and even, in his short photographic pieces, like a more formal Gary Snyder in Zen mode. The Jaccottet poems here are taken from *Words in the Air* (Gallery, 1998), a dual-language selection of his earlier work. He's one of the great names of modern French poetry. Houellebecq, on the other hand, is considered a poetry maverick in France, not a *real* poet properly speaking, in part because he speaks too properly. Despite the post-modern cityscapes and hip 'whatever' nihilism, he reads at times like a contemporary of Baudelaire, careful with his old-fashioned syllable count and rhetorical rhythms.

India's local languages are dying out one by one, to speak only of India. You sometimes get the erroneous impression, promoted by the globalization folks, that everyone everywhere is coming round to an Anglo-American norm. Robert Lowell, floating this idea in his introduction to *Imitations* (1961), made the startling claim that he was trying 'to do what my authors might have done if they were writing their poems now and in America' — which may in part explain the very uneven quality of that collection. If not poetry itself, in Bonnefoy's terms, 'the poetry' is indeed what gets lost, or rather hidden. 'The poetry' hides in its language of origin and is not finally translatable; we can only approximate. This being so, the best plan may be to approximate with zest, to refuse pedantry and intimidation. There's no reason to be shy of foreign authors who have probably done their own share of approximate translation, of adaptation.

Derek Mahon
2013

Index of Authors